CULTURE IS KING.

5 KEYS TO CREATE A HIGH-PERFORMING TEAM

COLLIN HENDERSON + KATE BETHELL

CONTENTS

INTRO

TOP-DOWN BOTTOM-UP

I'll never forget stepping over that line. It was a literal action with figurative ramifications that changed us.

It was my sophomore season on the Washington State University Cougar football team. We were stacked with talent, but we just weren't sealing the deal on some close wins. We lost three games in overtime and two games in the last minute. See what I mean?

Habits weren't changing the summer after that season, and some of my teammates and I had had enough. We were done with bad behavior and poor performance, and we weren't going to wait for one of our coaches to force a reset.

Sure, we had a lot of players who were interested. They liked what playing Division I football meant: wearing the crimson jersey and running out of the tunnel to screaming fans at Martin Stadium on Saturdays. But these guys weren't fully committed to the process or to each other, skipping workouts and taking off reps during weight training.

ARE YOU INTERESTED OR COMMITTED?

So the team leaders and I wanted to know who was all-in. We held a players-only meeting on the football field and asked the question, *"Are you interested or committed?"* Who would commit to this team and help develop a new culture? Who could we count on to create a collective unit that would stop losing and start winning? We believed excellence should be a lifestyle, not just saved for Saturdays. We didn't want it to be just some of us, we wanted it to be all of us. But we gave a choice: S*tep over this yard line on the football field or . . . don't. There's no gray area. You're in or you're not. You're either interested . . . or committed.*

We had a vision of excellence beginning with how we trained and practiced. We laid out the expectations: No one could miss a workout without giving notice. No leaving practice early. We needed to start behaving like the champions we wanted to be. And you know what? One by one, teammates crossed that line. Sure, maybe one or two didn't—I don't remember. All I can recall is the feeling, that energy shift. It was almost electric. The culture was changing. It set off a chain reaction that lead to three ten-win seasons for the Cougs. Was that an accident? I don't think so.

Don't get me wrong—we had a great coaching staff. But a collective team has more power than a coach. Than a leader. Than a manager. This doesn't just pertain to sports. This is life. **You don't need a title to be a leader.** Peer pressure goes both ways—it can be negative or positive. We had a few leaders on the team who wouldn't wait for the coach or the athletic director or anybody else to demand change. We took the ownership. We wanted to define our commitment level and support it with our actions. Period.

ARE YOU PROBLEM-BASED OR SOLUTION-BASED?

Years ago, I worked for a pharmaceuticals company selling a medication I actually used. I felt especially connected to my work because my mom and brother also took this product. While selling this medication, our company found ourselves in a bit of a predicament, resulting in a corporate integrity agreement with the FDA. Glossing over the complexities of the situation, I will tell you that our company was forced to change its business practices. We began following a patient-first model in which salespeople were paid based on a host of metrics rather than on their sales performances. Scores on verbal tests over the phone, written tests on the computer, and manager appraisals shaped the compensation structure.

Moving from a traditional sales structure to this was a humongous culture shift to say the least. I saw my teammates quoting problems but offering no solutions. For me, taking tests over the phone was a nightmare. I'd get anxiety and couldn't hardly speak. In addition to this culture shift, it's important to add (and you'll understand exactly why later in this book) that I did not enjoy working with some of my colleagues. I felt like I couldn't be myself and was forced to do things a certain way, which just added more stress to an already overwhelming situation.

I started noticing declines in my job performance, my satisfaction with the company, and my personal health. My blood pressure skyrocketed. This culture shift did not align with my skill set, but I was trying everything I could to fit the square peg into a round hole. I even took transcendental meditation and started seeing a counselor to try and lower my stress. I was not in an environment that was allowing me to thrive or do my best, and there was nothing I could do about it.

Ironically, I got chosen as a "Change Champion," a role in which I led workshops to educate other salespeople on navigating through feelings associated with change. My company even sent me to Philadelphia for a training on how to do this. I'd huddle small groups of a handful of people in hotel conference rooms or restaurant party rooms and enthusiastically present a slide deck explaining the change curve and how they should be handling this transition at work.

You guys, let me tell you, my spiel fell on deaf ears. People were slumped in their chairs with their arms folded across their chests. . .heavy frowns, furrowed brows—you get the idea. Nobody wanted to hear how they should be responding to a situation they felt like they had no control over. There was no autonomy or buy-in and certainly no room for feedback from employees. Every single person in these meetings aired complaints and problems but absolutely no solutions. There was no trust, little satisfaction, and low morale.

I can't say I blamed these people. I mean, I felt like a fraud myself! We, as employees, literally had zero control. And I certainly felt like I had no control over my happiness or my destiny with the company because of how it was structured. I just did not believe that what I was doing was making a difference, whether it was as a salesperson or as someone who was supposed to inspire morale and comfort with this mandated culture change. I was one of those metaphorical hamsters spinning on a wheel . . . going nowhere.

The thing is, **culture is established top-down, but lives bottom-up.** So, if the bottom doesn't align with the set values, then you can't sustain that culture. Said differently, one person—or in this case, a mandated shift in structure—can determine the culture, but if the people aren't buying in or thriving in that situation, the culture just won't succeed.

I knew myself well enough to know that my only option was to leave the company, and I know some other talented employees did, too. I couldn't focus on the unchangeable problems, only a solution for myself. Thankfully, I found a role elsewhere that met my needs and aligned with my strengths. And you know what? My growth and the empowerment from that situation and that shift created what I'm doing now—I wrote my first book, *Project Rise*, and my second, *Master Your Mindset*—and it set me on a completely different trajectory as a full time peak performance consultant and certified mental skills coach.

Do either of these examples of culture resonate with you (elite sports team or corporate life)? As an athlete, sales professional, and coach—whether in athletics or in mental performance—I've experienced an assortment of culture environments, from exceptional to terrible. I've also been called to lead in the same arenas, and though there are countless books and materials related to leadership, there are significantly fewer that directly pertain to building culture.

A 2015 study conducted by Duke University's Fuqua School of Business, in partnership with *CFO Magazine* and COLE, the Fuqua/Coach K Center on Leadership & Ethics found that only 15 percent of CEOs and CFOs said they thought their corporate culture is where it needs to be, which means **85 percent of CEOs and CFOs believe their culture is not where it needs to be**. Would you consider yourself in the same boat?

Let me take a second to define culture in my own terms. Plain and simple, **culture is the way and why we do things**. As these stories illustrate, you can turn a bad culture into a winning culture, though sometimes the culture itself is negative and won't change. It's all about the way things are done.

Exceptional leaders, whose organizations most certainly can be described as "winning," agree. Pastor Chad Veach who, along with wife Julia, leads Zoe Church in Los Angeles (Google this for some inspiration and a little visual of an amazing example of culture!) will tell you, "Culture is never what we say, it's always what we do . . . . Culture is unspoken."

TRANSFORMATION

So what if the culture seems great, yet there are no expectations or guidelines? Let me explain.

Football coach Keith Ross transformed the culture at Sumner High School in the Puget Sound area of Washington state (and yes, there will be plenty of examples of culture not relating to football or the state of Washington, I promise). Ross had been coaching for nearly twenty years years, but had been dominant only the last four. The thing is, he didn't know why or how. He called me and said, "Collin, we've had success, but I cannot define our culture." So, I asked him to have each of his coaches finish this sentence: "Sumner's culture can be defined by _____." Would it surprise you that each coach said something different? Completely different.

It's hard to scale culture unless all parties can clearly define what makes up their culture with key words, key actions, and key habits. Or you could say: **How we think, how we act, and how we treat each other.**

To take Sumner from a culture of ambiguousness to one of clarity, I led a culture workshop in three phases: with the coaching staff, with the seniors only, and with the entire team, and they clearly defined what their culture is all about. Coach Ross wanted to define the words, actions, and habits that would stand the test of time for his team. He asked his seniors to come up with their key phrase for the team, giving up control so they could own the culture at Sumner, just as my teammates and I did at Washington State.

Maybe they didn't know why they were winning before, but they certainly set a foundation for the next twenty years. In case you're curious, Ross and his staff chose the phrase "Do your job," while the seniors' slogan was "Set a New Standard" (#SANS). They collectively chose the following team values: Impact, Improve, and Influence the Valley (the community where they live).

Through self-evaluation, Ross said he used to be more of a volatile coach, with self-validation coming from wins and losses. He still cares about winning, of course, but now he values developing his players into stand-up young men. One way the Sumner football program fosters this development is through blurring the lines between teams (freshman, junior varsity, and varsity) by meeting together as a unit. They also share team dinners as a large group, ensuring everyone is equally important.

You can't have a culture unless you're committed and not just interested. You must be solution-based instead of problem-based. And you better believe you've got to be open to a great transformation. In *Culture is King*, you'll learn why you don't have to have a title to be a leader or create culture. You'll learn how a simple equation can lead to incredible transformation for your team: the power of **genuine connection** (relationships) along with **trust** . . . combined with **vulnerability**. I'll dive deep into these topics, and give you examples of the equation in action. I'll also arm you with the **FIVE KEYS** to elevating connection, trust, and vulnerability within your team or organization to create winning culture.

Looking for a sneak peek at these keys? They are as follows:

1. ENERGY
2. VISION
3. STANDARDS
4. LANGUAGE
5. LEGACY

Have you ever driven a country road and seen a beautiful, old thriving tree in the middle of a field? A winning culture is like this picturesque tree.

ENERGY is like the sun that shines upon the tree and the rain that soaks its roots. Without these, a tree would not grow; its buds wouldn't blossom. Similarly, without energy . . . I almost want to say, "What's the point?" Energy brings life to the lifeless and inspires the uninspired.

VISION is like the top branches of the tree. How high can your organization reach? How big can you dream?

STANDARDS are like the roots of the tree. These are the core beliefs your organization stands upon—the grounding elements that hold it in place.

LANGUAGE is like the leaves that provide shade in the summer, gorgeous colors in the fall, disappear in the winter, and signal new life in the spring. Leaves can be taken for granted, but without them, trees wouldn't survive—they help trees make food and stay alive. Positive language, words, and communication create a sort of vitality among your group.

LEGACY is just like the rings around a tree trunk. How long is what you've created as a leader going to live? Will you help produce a stunning, thriving tree that will be a beacon in an empty field?

Between topics, I'll share with you what I call "Culture Case Studies." These stories address real-life situations of positive cultures and examine the outcomes on the people involved. Maybe you can relate to one of these stories and use the information to help outline what makes up your current culture and how you want to either enforce or change it. I'll also sprinkle in wisdom from some outstanding leaders from various industries ranging from sports to corporations. Some of these people are my friends, while others are inspirational thought leaders in their fields, and still others are people I've worked with as a mental performance coach. I'm excited to spread their experiences and knowledge with you.

Are you ready to dig into the material? Don't forget to have a pen and highlighter handy while you read. I'll ask a lot of questions you'll want to thoughtfully consider as you lead and build culture within your organization.

CHAPTER ONE

TRANSFOR-MATION

"If you want to be great and successful, choose people who are great and successful and walk side by side with them." — Ralph Waldo Emerson

Let's start with the end in mind: Good cultures exhibit **connection** and **trust**, and it all starts with fostering positive relationships. When you're able to do this authentically, and when you show up as your true self, you'll be able to build a culture that promotes **vulnerability**. That is, those you lead will feel valued for being who they truly are. When combined, these ingredients will magically inspire **transformation**. It's a three-step process and a bit of an equation—whatever you want to call it, the benefits compound. Step 1: Create connection. Step 2: Build trust. Step 3: Model and inspire vulnerability. Step 4: Witness transformation.

CONNECTION

The importance of relationships isn't just something I've witnessed in my decades as an athlete, business professional, and through my personal experiences—it's fact. In 1938, researchers at Harvard started studying sophomore male students with the hope of finding the key to happiness in life. The Harvard Study of Adult Development followed more than 250 males throughout their lives. A large handful of these men are still alive and continue to be studied, as do their offspring. The study has transformed over time, but the key findings haven't: **Health and happiness are related to strength of close relationships.** Of course this is extremely generalized, but the decades of research continue to reveal that it's not money or a title, it's the relationships you have and the connections you make that lead to happiness.

I've worked with a lot of teams over the years, but the one that comes to mind when I think about the Harvard study and the impact of relationships is the Miami University hockey team. A perennial powerhouse in collegiate hockey, the RedHawks have had numerous winning seasons and are currently under the direction of the winningest coach in school history, Enrico Blasi. Blasi has been at the helm for twenty years and was a player himself. If you want to talk about winning cultures, let's talk about Blasi and what he's done with the RedHawks. For him, it's all about one word: **brotherhood**.

I had the opportunity to spend time with the RedHawks, fully entrenched in the brotherhood on campus for a day. I met with coaches, captains, and the whole team, working on mental skills, and, quite honestly, submerging myself into this rich culture and tradition. A camera was on campus at the same time, as part of a YouTube mini-series called "The Season" (filmed by my dear friend and Emmy Award-winning filmmaker, Jason Johnson), which followed Blasi's team through the 2018-2019 season (you can catch me in action in the fourth installment of "The Season"). The first episode begins with Blasi opening the door to his team culture by saying the brotherhood is not about hockey.

"I've never been one to say, 'Hey, we want to make the national tournament or win a championship or anything like that,'" he said. "I think those are all things that, in the back of your mind, you always think about. I think you have that goal. But my expectation is that every day, we come to the rink . . . every day we do anything—off the ice, on the ice, in the classroom—we do it to the best of our ability, and we push ourselves to be better, and we hold ourselves accountable."

Expectations and accountability are just a few of the values expressed in the brotherhood, something so special and unique to this hockey team that it's kept two current seniors on the rink in Miami instead of going pro after their junior seasons. They want to win a championship, yes, but a legacy of leaving the program better than they found it is more profound. The players are all in with this philosophy . . . this credo . . . this way of life. And it's a great contrast to the short words and phrases some teams use to define their culture. Read it for yourself and tell me you don't feel inspired or like you want to borrow a line or two. You guys, I know this is lengthy, but it's so powerful I wanted to include it. Get your highlighter out, and do not skip over this!

THE BROTHERHOOD

As a brother, I build unity within the program.
I make it clear in word and action that I can be trusted.
I am unselfish and make sacrifices for the good of the team.
I prepare my body for the competition and engage in social habits that optimize my performance.
I know that I have the power to support and strengthen every other member of our family.

I embody the high standards of the program in everything I do and in how I present myself.
I look in the mirror before pointing out the faults in someone else.
I respect how we are different and how we are the same.
I take great pride in the accomplishments of every member of the program.
I am accountable to you . . . and to myself.
I will not allow your reputation to be tainted.
I will have the courage to have the tough conversations.
I will take the time to know your dreams and passions. I will do what I can to help make them come true.
I care about my performance in the classroom.
I know that my actions in the community reflect on our entire program.
I will stand up for what is right.
I go to you rather than around you.
I build bridges . . . not walls.
I know how to forgive.
I take responsibility for being better tomorrow than I am today.
I know when to lead and when to follow.
I will do the hard things daily that translate into a championship culture.
I will leave this program better than when I found it.
As brothers, we share a lifetime bond that I will cherish forever.
And as your brother, I know that I am a champion!

Wow, right? The brotherhood. It's about connection. It's about trust. It's a solid high-performing culture.

And what about you? Have you ever been a part of a team like this? Think about the organizations you've been a part of, whether at work or in sports or maybe even at your church. I'm sure there are some good and some bad in the mix. **What were the traits you can name that made those positive cultures stand out? Chances are connection and trust are among the top of the list.**

TRUST

Let's talk a little more about trust. Just like relationships, trust has actually been studied as it pertains to happiness and success. Through his work studying neuroscience relating to high-performing organizations, scientist and author Paul J. Zak concluded a "culture of trust" really does matter.

"In my research I've found that building a culture of trust is what makes a meaningful difference," Zak said in a Harvard Business Review article. "Employees in high-trust organizations are more productive, have more energy at work, collaborate better with their colleagues, and stay with their employers longer than people working at low-trust companies. They also suffer less chronic stress and are happier with their lives, and these factors fuel stronger performance."

To show you the specifics, here's what that whittles down to in numbers:

"Compared with people at low-trust companies, people at high-trust companies report: 74 percent less stress, 106 percent more energy at work, 50 percent higher productivity, 13 percent fewer sick days, 76 percent more engagement, 29 percent more satisfaction with their lives, 40 percent less burnout."
—Harvard Business Review

In 2017, I experienced growth from all angles, and I lived these positive statistics. I worked my tail off to be number one in the country for sales growth within my company. We also welcomed our fourth child. And I published my first book, *Project Rise*, that fall. To say it was a big year would be an understatement. But none of it would have been possible (except the baby!) without the connections formed within and support from my company.

At the beginning of the year, our national sales director, Tom Couture, pulled me aside and said, "Collin, I'm going to support you in whatever makes you happy." He said it didn't matter if it was at our company or elsewhere. "I care about you as a person," he said. I can close my eyes and feel just how comforting and sincere those words felt. He knew I was setting up speaking and coaching engagements but instead of saying, "You better focus on your day job," he gave me the trust to hit my numbers and the encouragement to succeed in other endeavors. So I set about my business, working hard to try and be number one, feeling completely supported.

As the year wrapped up, my colleagues and I traveled to the elaborate national sales meeting honoring all of the top performers from across the United States. You guys, this is like the Oscars for the salespeople within my company. No one knows exactly who will win the award for top producer, so you can imagine the state of shock I was in when I heard my wife and kids' voices come over the speakers and their faces appear on the big screen in this ballroom. They knew I won and secretly recorded a congratulatory message for me. Tears streamed down my face like a baby. As soon as I pulled it together, I had the amazing opportunity to address my colleagues. And guess what? The man who welcomed me to the stage was the same director who told me he supported me no matter what . . . almost a year to the day before this. I can't think of a finer example of trust in action.

When I got on stage to speak to 400 of my colleagues, I started thanking people and began outlining my values: gratitude, giving, and growing. After that, the president of my division summarized my speech with those three keys and, get this . . . he bought my book for every single person in attendance. Literally one hour later, his assistant sent me an order for 500 copies. Now, you can't tell me that's not a legitimate work culture! They trusted me and give me the autonomy to get my job done and support me in my business as a peak performance coach. And I could go on and on about the relationships I've formed while working for this company—some of my best friends are my colleagues. It's an incredible feeling when you have positive relationships coupled with trust pouring out from your employer.

My employer valued who I was as a person, something Julie M. said should be a top priority for leaders. Julie M. is a human resources director at a Fortune 500 company. She's been with the company for decades and has seen it grow from a small business to an industry-leader, witnessing incredible growth and change. She knows what successful culture looks like. "For me, culture is tied around behaviors—in winning cultures, when people can show up as they truly are, that creates inclusion, authenticity, trust, and they can speak their truth. And it sounds maybe a little corny, but when you can do that, I've seen people move mountains. You can do just about anything."

It's one thing to say you want to help others show up as they truly are, but how exactly do you go about doing that? It starts with courage and then the ball starts really rolling with the addition of vulnerability.

VULNERABILITY

Certified high performance coach and guru in the personal development field, Brendon Burchard, said, "Courage is the cornerstone habit of high performance." In addition to this, the great Brené Brown, research professor and well-known expert on all things related to the topic of vulnerability, said that every act of courage involves vulnerability. Consider these beliefs, and you'll start to understand why letting your guard down, and inspiring others to do so, too, truly leads to transformation. "Authenticity" and "vulnerability" are such buzzwords right now, but there's a reason. Especially in an age of social media and limited privacy, it's absolutely vital leaders encourage these traits.

I can think of no better example of someone showing up as they truly are than my college baseball coach, Tim Mooney. The interesting thing is that never in a million years would I have said this unless I had the opportunity to work with him as a professional, after I graduated. As a player, I would have described Mooney as a rigid, old-school type of coach. He rarely showed any emotion. I would say he cared about me as a player first. He didn't express how he may have cared about me as a person. Even as I write these words, they sound so harsh, and that's not at all how I think about him or his legacy now.

Mooney had tremendous success as an NAIA coach at Albertson College in Idaho, winning nearly 70 percent of his games and racking up a national title before taking over at WSU. But he just didn't have the same success until his fourth season with the Cougars, and by then, the athletic director had already decided to let Mooney go. I think this is unfortunate because I started to see some changes in Mooney at this point. He took our team on a retreat that season, and we didn't focus on baseball at all. Rather, we worked on team-building the entire weekend. I saw him trying to connect and create relationships with players, growing as a leader and a coach at the highest collegiate level. But as I said, it was too late since he stepped down after that season (which, coincidentally, ended up being the first winning season in ten years for the Cougs).

After I completed my undergraduate work, while starting my master's degree, I took a graduate position in the athletic department foundation office. Imagine my surprise when Mooney started a job in the same department, with a desk right next to mine. I can tell you I wasn't excited.

But something fascinating happened when he wasn't coaching. It was like he had a completely different personality. As a player, I don't think he even knew my major or that I had a brother. But before he even sat down at his desk he asked me how school was going for me and about my parents. As time went on, we started going to lunch together. We developed a new relationship. He seemed to thrive in this new environment, with an uplifting personality, and he was great at his job. It was like a complete 180-degree turn from the man I knew as Coach Mooney to the friend I had in my coworker, Tim.

During our time working together and because I had graduated, most of my friends moved away. I went through a horrible breakup during this time, and you know who I turned to? Tim Mooney. He cared about me so much as a person. We built connection and trust working together, and he was vulnerable in showing his true self to me and vice-versa. Though my life has taken many twists and turns since our time together, we still keep in touch. He is thriving in his current position at another major university. But to this day, I truly believe if he had approached coaching with the mentality he did when we worked together ("I care about you as a person first and a player/professional second"), he might still be in the coaching profession. Yet, maybe it's just that his authentic self is best served as an administrator and world class fundraiser.

As a leader, if you yourself are open to transformation, and if you feel your organization is in need of a bit of a transformation even before focusing on the five keys of culture, then start here, with these areas: connection, trust, and vulnerability. **Take some time to think about how you approach those you lead. Are you thinking about their personal success ahead of yours? Do they trust you? Do you have an open-door policy? And how do you show up each day? Do you try to cover up your flaws or do you share the things you struggle with?** I'm not saying you need to broadcast everything or air all of your dirty laundry, but letting others in encourages them to be open and honest and able to express their needs, desires, and dreams.

Vulnerability added to the powers of connection and trust fuels positive cultures in an almost magical way. It doesn't matter if it's a small hockey team or a large corporation or even a workplace friendship. But as they say, Rome wasn't built in a day, and neither is this type of environment. It takes work, and it takes time. And there are many ways a positive culture can be broken or sabotaged.

CULTURE KILLERS

In my research and experience, I've identified six common setbacks, or "Culture Killers" as I call them, to be aware of in your quest to create a winning culture. I'm sure you are familiar with all of these:

EGO — *It's all about "me!"* When one person or a group of people care more about who gets the credit than in a "team-first" philosophy.

COMPARISON — When someone wants others to fail so that they can excel, ignoring the old adage that "a rising tide lifts all ships."

EXCUSES — When people in your organization justify, defend, or rationalize negative actions or behaviors, believing them to be acceptable rather than taking ownership. Excuses are issued when rules, values, or even trust is broken. Excuses are like a virus that can infect and negatively affect a team.

LAZINESS — A lack of buy-in. You can also file "apathy" under this Culture Killer—when people don't show up or they have a complete lack of commitment. When someone is interested and not committed (as demonstrated in the introduction).

LACK OF COMMUNICATION — When there's assumptions or insufficient communication on one end, it affects the giver and the receiver. Communication is a two-way street.

LACK OF TRUST — When someone does not sincerely trust the intent or integrity of the leader or the organization, then it's virtually impossible to reach consistent success.

Which one of these Culture Killers speaks to you regarding your team or organization? You might even have one or two additional "killers" you can add to this list. Don't despair, however. I'm going to empower you with information and tactics to negate these interruptions and set you on the right path.

Without further adieu, let's start exploring the FIVE KEYS to elevating connection, trust, and vulnerability within your team or organization so you, too, can help foster a winning culture.

CHAPTER TWO
ENERGY

"Energy and persistence conquer all things." — *Benjamin Franklin*

A few years back, I spent time in Boise, Idaho for work. I was near a Starbucks en route to see a customer and called to see about bringing drinks for everyone. Though super thankful, this customer said, "You know, we all really like Dutch Bros., if you wouldn't mind swinging through there instead." A little dumbfounded I said, "Dutch Bros.? Is that a furniture store? What the heck is Dutch Bros.?" Being from Seattle I thought, *How dare you talk about any other coffee shop but Starbucks.* But I figured they asked for it, and I was going to deliver.

So I put Dutch Bros. in my GPS and pulled up to this little shack adorned in a Dutch motif with windmills and tulips. I was still a little uncertain about this so-called coffee shop and sorely disappointed in the length of the car lineup. Not just that, but there was an employee greeting cars with an iPad, chatting about orders and offering suggestions. This is go-

23

ing to take forever, I thought. Except it didn't.

A little backstory for you: At this point in my life, I never drank coffee. I didn't like the taste and could never really find a drink I liked, so I just didn't drink coffee.

Somehow, the cars whipped through the line, and it was my turn faster than I imagined. The employee approached me with the biggest smile on his face, seemingly on a caffeine high. He asked me how my day was, and he just seemed so happy. I was a little like, *I don't know what's going on here, but I'll go along with it.* I told him it was my first time in Boise, and I repeated the handful of drinks for my customer. Then he asked me what I wanted to drink. He said since it was my first time, my drink was on the house. Nervously, I told him I didn't drink coffee. But it was like he didn't hear that because he proceeded to ask me what my favorite drink was, to which I said, "a chocolate milkshake."

"Well, we don't have chocolate milkshakes," he said, "but how about we make an iced mocha for you, and since you don't love the taste of coffee, instead of two shots of espresso, we'll use just one."

I wasn't so sure about that, but I said I was down for anything. It was a free drink, afterall. I didn't like coffee, but I thought I'd give it a try, and let me tell you . . . the minute that drink hit my lips it was like the heavens opened up, doves went flying, and a choir of angels sang in the clouds. It just tasted SO. GOOD. In that moment, I became a coffee drinker.

Let's review: Dutch Bros. had great music blaring when I pulled up. Then, an employee with a big grin and a fantastic attitude not only greeted me, but found out it was my first time in Boise, and offered me a free drink, which they perfectly concocted after asking me just a couple of personal preference questions. The energy of this entire experience was off the charts.

I hate to put down Starbucks as I'm a Seattle kid . . . but Starbucks never asked me about what I wanted or gave me a free drink, you know? And now I drink coffee pretty much every day because of that one experience. Plus, I'll go out of my way to drive through a Dutch Bros. simply because of the energy. The **energy**! It was so welcoming, contagious, and engaging.

ENERGY = FOUNDATION

You may have heard this in an elementary science class, but it's important: Every living being is made up of two things: matter and energy. Energy is the foundation of success. Think about good teams or good environments or people you like to be around. Does the room light up when they enter? How about when you enter or leave a room? Think about that one. Are you an energy-maker or an energy-taker?

THE RULE OF ONE-THIRD

Think of a simple pie chart adding up to 100 percent. There are three types of people on any team or in any organization. You are one of these three, so keep that in mind as I walk through the slices of the pie.

One third of the pie, or roughly 33 percent, is made up of **ENERGY ZOMBIES.** These people have a pulse, but no passion. They go through the motions. They say the worst four-letter word, according to best-selling author and peak performance speaker Mel Robbins, which is "fine." As in, "I'm FINE." Ugh. You know the type. They lack passion. They're not engaged. They're probably scrolling on their phones instead of paying attention. They're zombies! If you looked at the bell curve, they are classically right in the middle. They just show up. They don't really complain, but they don't offer solutions. They're just kind of there. Can you think of any co-workers or teammates that fit this mold?

The next third, or about 33 percent, are—to coin a phrase from author/speaker Jon Gordon—**ENERGY VAMPIRES**. These people suck the energy right out of the room. They are problem-based, or as I like to say, they BCS: Blame, Complain, and Shame. They have an excuse for everything. They have poor body language. Maybe they're always slumped over, moping around, or living with resting bitch face (yes, I said it!). Do you know anybody who just has bad body language?

The final third, or close to 33 percent, are **ENERGY HEROES.** Who doesn't want to be a hero? These folks are the other end of the bell curve from those vampires. They are committed, solution-based, and eager to connect to others. They want to be the best they can be, offer trust, and see their group or team rise to the top.

Motivationally speaking, there are four types of people, driven by one of the following forces: fear, incentives, self (meaning they are intrinsically motivated), or pro-social (meaning they're motivated to contribute to something bigger than themself). Which type do you think are the heroes? The heroes are those who are intrinsically driven and who have a prosocial motivation—they want to create an impact and do something positive.

Now, at this point, we're going to eliminate the zombies and the vampires, and talk more about coaching up the heroes in your group. Yes, it's important to touch upon what to do about the negative characters lurking, as inevitably they play a part in your culture, but let's first focus on the positive. *(I'll teach you more about dealing with the negative later in this chapter, as well as in Chapter 5, which is all about LANGUAGE.)*

FEELINGS, ADVERSITY, AND TIME

There are three challenges to energy—to being your best and fulfilling what you set out to do: 1) feelings, 2) adversity, and 3) time.

To exemplify these three challenges, let's get back to the numbers and stick with the pie analogy. The heroes represent 33 percent of the pie, yes. One-third of these people decide they just don't fee 1 like doing whatever it is they need to do to achieve a goal or follow-through on a task. They let their **FEELINGS** dictate their behavior and action.

You can think about it this way: Say you go to church Sunday, you hear the sermon, and you leave so fired up. You're going to take that message right into your week and be a better person, changing lives of those around you Monday through the following Sunday. But . . . there's a problem. You miss your alarm clock the next day, and suddenly your best intentions fly right out the window, and you're cutting people off on your way to work, stealing a parking spot, and cutting in the coffee line en route to your desk at work. You're no longer living in the peak state you were when you left church yesterday. You just don't FEEL like making the change you hoped. You go back to your old ways. Your feelings lied to you. You lost your energy because you didn't feel like it.

All right. Now, another third of this shrinking pie are going to drop out because of the second challenge of **ADVERSITY**. Whether it's bad timing in the market, you fail, or someone on your team making a crucial mistake, or a co-worker you really rely on at work screwing up a joint project, these things are inevitable. Adversity is always lurking, and challenges are never going away. When faced with these things, some people are going to crumble and stop. Their energy just falls by the wayside because they are not getting the result they hoped in return. These people give up.

27

Cut off a final third of this tiny sliver of pie left to represent the heroes who run into the final challenge of energy and peak performance, which is **TIME**. Can you sustain that level of commitment of energy for not just one week, one quarter, or one year . . . but for the long haul? This comes down to grit, folks. (Or, as grit expert, psychologist and author Angela Duckworth, says, "when passion and perseverance meet.") Can you stick with it?

Whenever I get discouraged in this arena—when I want to see results sooner than I do or when I waver in any pursuit after a certain amount of time, I like to think of the litany of famous people who had and have grit. Here are a handful of truly gritty examples:

- **Jeff Bezos**, founder of Amazon, didn't make a profit until year five.
- **FedEx** didn't turn a profit until year four.
- **Abraham Lincoln** lost eight elections. EIGHT!
- **Stephen Curry** didn't make the all-star team in the NBA until five years in.

Are you reading these examples, people? You have to stick with it.

NOW, there's barely any pie left. In fact, we're left with just **1 percent** of the energy heroes. Why is that 1 percent so important? Well, according to NCAA.org, only about 2 percent of high school athletes get a scholarship, and of all the sports that have a draft, only about 1 percent of those athletes get drafted, with baseball being the exception (close to 10 percent of baseball athletes get drafted). Aside from sports, according to CNBC, 1 percent of the world's population owns half of the world's wealth. Did you know that? Isn't that crazy to think about? The 1 percent in these two examples is able to survive those three challenges of feelings, adversity, and time.

Do you want a couple of specific examples of this? Well, here you go: "The Oracle of Omaha," Warren Buffett. He had a paper route before he was ten, made his first investment at age eleven, and filed his first tax return as a teenager. Basically, he was working straight out of the womb. **Feelings** did not get in the way of his actions. He worked hard always despite how he felt. How about **adversity**? In the 1970s, he lost more than half of his wealth because of bad investments and also because the stock market tanked. And **time**? Buffett accrued 99 percent of his income after the age of fifty.

And let's talk more about Steph Curry. He was not offered a scholarship at a major Division I university. He grew up in North Carolina, and none of the famed schools in state offered him a chance (think: NC, NC State, Duke). Davidson College (with a student population of less than 2,000) in North Carolina, however, did offer Curry a scholarship. Curry could have said, "I don't **feel** like playing at Davidson because I can't make it to the NCAA tournament or get drafted out of this college," but he didn't. He kept grinding and competing, and he took Davidson to the Elite Eight, and he got drafted seventh overall. What about **adversity**? In his third and fourth year in the league, he didn't even play more than half a season because of ankle injuries. He could have chalked it up to bad luck and given up. And **time**? I already mentioned this, but Curry was not an all-star in the NBA until year FIVE. No one really talked about him once he got to the league, but he kept working hard, and is now often referred to as one of the greatest shooters of all-time in the NBA.

Life is about energy. Feelings, adversity, and time are the questions in the test we call life. We must overcome these obstacles to create winning culture. There's nothing fancy. Trust me, you're going to want to wake up and hit snooze. You are. You're going to fail. There's going to be mental and physical endurance tests, and you're going to need to put in the time.

There are no shortcuts.

USING YOUR NATURAL RESOURCES

Just as water, oxygen, and oil are natural resources, we, as humans, have natural resources—or sources of energy—at our disposal. In studying and teaching peak performance, I've boiled it down to three: **playing to your strengths, knowing your why, and working with others.**

PLAYING TO YOUR STRENGTHS

Playing to your strengths is not just about what you're good at, but what you love to do. If you have enough self-awareness to really know what you're good at, then that's going to help you stay in the game. If you're in a role that feels awkward or that's affecting you mentally or even physically (like the job I was stuck in that stressed me out beyond explanation), then you're not in your lane, playing to your strengths.

Think about Target. This store has everything a mom could want or need all in one place. And how about Nordstrom? Nordstrom offers personal shopping-type customer service to everyone. You know the kind of customer service you're going to get when walking into a Nordstrom. I'm sure you could think of a few more examples of stores or shopping experiences that play to a company's strengths.

What about you personally? Are you playing to your strengths in life? There's a little saying I like to rattle off when I'm speaking to a group that directly relates to this energy source of playing to your strengths: **"Scratch an itch. Find a niche. You'll be rich, bitch!"** (Of course, depending on the audience, I add the "bitch" part in there only to hammer home the point and get a laugh, so don't repeat that unless you feel your audience can laugh along with you!) Unless you're born with a trust fund, you're going to have to work to earn money, right? So why not follow this prescription?

The first thing is *scratching an itch*. What lights you up? What role or skillset gives you energy? I say follow your curiosity or passion. For example, author Elizabeth Gilbert, who wrote the wildly famous *Eat, Pray, Love: One Woman's Search for Everything Across Italy, India and Indonesia*, did just this. People pestered her, wondering what her sequel would be about, and instead of getting hung up on the topic, she decided just to keep writing about herself and her curiosities and followed up with a book about her life after *Eat, Pray, Love*.

Next part. *What's a niche you can bring value to?* Where is there a need? This one's easy for me to explain because I'm living it right now. I resigned from my "day job" doing medical device sales and have made a career as a performance coach and mindset consultant. I specialize in businesses, athletes and schools - all areas of past experience.

The more niche, the better . . . the more specified in your skillset, the better. When you are playing to your strengths in something specific that fires you up like nobody else, well, *you'll be rich* in energy, in joy, and you'll probably make money, too, because you'll be doing something that's so fulfilling. You know what they say, "Do what you love, and you'll never work a day in your life."

Stop and think about yourself first. Are you grinding or are you grooving? How about those on your team? Are they working or performing to the best of their abilities in their roles? Really think about this. If you're coaching a basketball player who might not always score or rebound but who consistently and reliably brings instant energy off hustle plays no matter when he enters the game, make sure he knows that's his special gift and how much you value him because of it. Take the time to build on the unique strengths of everyone in your group, and you will be amazed at the results.

KNOWING YOUR "WHY"

The second source of energy is knowing your "why." Simply put, this means understanding the meaning behind what you're doing. It could be from a place of pain or a place of joy. It could be a person or relationship. Truly understanding and honoring the reasons and motivations behind your actions is allowing a special light to shine in your life. If you're working or playing a sport or contributing to any type of organization, and there's no meaning behind your work, you can't do something truly great.

If you need a deeper understanding of this concept and haven't read the book *Man's Search for Meaning*, by Viktor Frankl, I recommend it. During WWII, Nazis captured Frankl, a Jewish psychiatrist, and his family. Frankl analyzed the Holocaust and basically had an epiphany that if you didn't have a "why," or a meaning, then you'd die. As an example, Frankl said the holidays were a truly trying time, with higher mortality rates, because people hoped they would be saved by the holidays, and when they weren't, many gave up hope. Conversely, he saw people who had something to stay alive for—whether that be a career or a marriage or children or something outside that they hadn't finished yet—would stay alive. **They had something other than themselves.**

I'll give you another example of uncovering the "why" pertaining to sports. I completed a program called "Finding Your Best" by Pete Carroll and psychologist Michael Gervais, which, as the name implies, includes courses on working toward becoming your best. One of the sessions featured an interview between Carroll and Courtney Thompson, who was an Olympic volleyball player and now a mindset coach. Thompson was a setter at University of Washington and went on to play professionally. She shared a story about her time as a pro when one of her teammates, an outside hitter, just never smiled. This teammate kind of moped around and seemed a bit disinterested. It looked as though there was no joy or love for the game with this teammate, so Thompson decided to ask her why she even played in an attempt to tap into her potential and perhaps make her come more alive. The teammate said she played for the money, to support her poor family. She shared if she didn't play well or their team didn't do well, then her family didn't have the money. So Thompson suggested the hitter make a gesture to her family whenever she did well, something that also garnered a smile. So, after a point or a save, the hitter started motioning with a fist-pump "cha-CHING" as a way of saying, "Money in the bank for my family!" This player's "why" was her family, and **by uncovering and acknowledging this why, it brought the player and the teammates much more energy and joy.**

WORKING WITH OTHERS

These sources of energy are SUPER POWERS. We all have these natural resources within us: playing to your strengths, uncovering your why, and finally, working with others. I like to say the term "LET'S GO" instead of "working together," because it just packs more of a punch and means exactly what it says. "Let's go" is plural. It's not "I go," or "me go," or even "you go." It's "let's go." Let US go. Do things in relation to others. Together. Connected. Think back to that Harvard study explained in the first chapter of this book. There's a natural energy when we're connected as a team, and working together.

Again, let's check in with some real world examples: Look at Nike. You've got Phil Knight and Bill Bowerman. And how about Microsoft? Paul Allen and Bill Gates. Apple? Steve Jobs and Steve Wozniak. Most of the massive companies of the world that have brought true value to you and me likely have two or more partners behind the story. And if you want to circle back to the Jeff Bezos Amazon example . . . well, his parents gave him their life savings. He didn't do it all on his own.

How you get energy is by living in communion with others rather than living in a silo. So, as you manage your group or lead your team, think about pairing people up, helping them find a buddy or a mentor. The point is that no one should do it alone. This simple act will create energy, I promise. There's so much power in a group—it's a fact. Psychologists call this the "Kohler Effect," in which people tend to work harder when they are pushed in a group setting.

Here's another example for you. Over the years, I've tried to do a podcast. It's something I've always wanted to do as a way to get my message out there in a different medium. I did five episodes on my own, and then I just couldn't sustain the effort. At the same time, I was meeting in a small group with a bunch of high schoolers weekly. One of our lessons was about serving. We got to talking about how we could spread the knowledge from our meetings beyond the group that sat in front of us. One of the student-athletes in attendance, Tanner, who is super into leadership and studying broadcast journalism, enthusiastically said, "We should start a podcast! Everyone in the world could hear our lessons."

I told him the two of us could take this on, but that he'd have to produce it and that I would just show up. Tanner wants to be an announcer, so practicing speaking into a microphone really motivated him. When we paired my desire with his, we started recording episode after episode simply because we did it TOGETHER. As I write this book, we've recorded more than 70 episodes, and we're not stopping. We hold each other accountable and certainly play to our strengths. I deliver the content, but Tanner does the write-ups, production, music, and links it all up to social media platforms magically. He even made a studio with foam soundboards, chairs for when we have guests, and microphones. Coincidentally our first episode was, "What's Our Why?" His why is leadership and broadcasting. My why is that I struggled with my confidence and mindset . . . and I'm an author, but not everyone reads, so I wanted to get this content out in different ways. I failed when I tried to do a podcast alone. It was just me. But when I had someone to do it with, WE succeeded. We both achieved, and Tanner even has a broadcast resume now before finishing high school.

Let's recap, shall we? There are three "resources" in the human condition from which you gain energy: playing to your strengths, knowing your why, and working with others (being connected rather than alone). Everything on earth starts and ends with energy. Period. If you don't take ownership of your energy, you will not survive.

I'd be remiss if I didn't mention one element, which I'd hope you've considered but feel as though I must spell out in case you haven't, and that's FUN. Think of some of the best teams you've been a part of. I'm going to wager you had a lot of fun, right? Especially if you're grinding toward a goal, you must take the time to have fun. As a leader, are you intentional about creating an environment in which fun is fostered? I mentioned Zoe Church earlier, and maybe you don't necessarily associate "church" with "fun," but perhaps you should, because it definitely works for this church. Pastor Julia Veach said the "fun element" is a key element in their culture. "[It's] enjoying whatever we do and partying with a purpose. We actually intentionally party with a purpose. We celebrate the wins, we laugh through the failures. Fun is absolutely a part of it."

When I'm coaching people regarding mindset training, we talk about energy and fun all the time. I used to talk more about goals, actions, habits, and creating a personal philosophy. But now I focus a ton on energy first because energy drives all those other things. It's like fuel. And if you aren't having fun, then why are you doing what you're doing? Life's too short!

What's YOUR energy source? What brings you joy? Is it qual-ity time with others or spending time alone? Stop and think about these things. Write them down. Encourage your team members or your group to do the same. You need energy to tackle the obstacles along the way and to lift up those around you. And if you're feeling like your energy is low . . . well, go back to your list, dabble in a little self-care, get some sleep, and then show up. Because a sail needs wind. Humans need food. Cars don't go if they don't have gas. Likewise, you can't sustain great culture if energy isn't at the center.

WHO: Bryan Reynolds

WHAT: Anthem Coffee

WHERE: Puyallup/Tacoma, Washington

WHY & HOW: Not every coffee shop you pop into has a written mission statement, vision, and values, but with Anthem Coffee, you'll find each of these proudly displayed on its website and lived out in the experience you'll receive walking through the door at any of the six Anthem locations. With a mission of "heroic hospitality," and the motto "live loud," Anthem Coffee, led by co-founder Bryan Reynolds, is incredibly intentional about serving customers and inspiring them to "win at life." Reynolds proudly hires based on "fit" first and then trains the skills needed to succeed in the job. He asks employees what they hope to get out of their employment and how he can help them achieve their goals or "fuel their 'why,'" as he says.

Reynolds is a student and practitioner of servant leadership, constantly asking himself, "What can I take off your plate so you can rise higher?" Perhaps most admirable, however, is Reynolds' ability to honestly share his failures and shortcomings as a leader, especially when the business was in its infancy. After much trial and error, Reynolds is confident in his recipes for success, whether in creating culture, leading a team, or whipping up a latte. First, "figure out what your guiding principles are or 'this is how we do what we do here' . . . and live by the guiding principles you set in place because it will keep you from burning out, and that's crucial," Reynolds said. Then, know your truths as a leader.

For Reynolds, it's the following:
1. Leadership begins with you.
2. Leaders love and serve.
3. Leaders stay coachable and teachable.
4. Leaders stay present where they're planted.

Do any of these leadership keys speak to you? What would you add? When you're hiring or recruiting, what do you look for—someone who can perform certain skills or someone who fits your vision and values and can be taught the skills needed to be successful in his or her position?

LEARN MORE ABOUT BRYAN REYNOLDS and ANTHEM COFFEE: myanthemcoffee.com

CHAPTER THREE
VISION

"Make your vision so clear that your fears become irrelevant." —Anonymous

If I say the word "Starbucks," what do you think of? Chances are you think of white paper cups with a simple green logo, friends drinking coffee and catching up in comfy chairs, or colleagues meeting to discuss business with laptops and lattes. But did you know when Starbucks first opened, it merely sold coffee beans and not piping hot cups of Joe? Former CEO, Howard Schultz, worked for Starbucks when there were just four stores. He traveled to Italy on a business trip where his inspiration and vision for what Starbucks could be emerged. He saw coffee as a ritual and coffee shops as places where people could meet and mingle away from home or work. He called this the "third place," a vision for future Starbucks stores, and something every Starbucks strives to be for customers to this day.

Schultz stepped down as CEO in 2000, and when he was away, Starbucks' vision changed. It became a retail shop of sorts, selling more than just pastries to accompany coffee, things like warm breakfast sandwiches, and CDs (remember those?) among other non-coffee-related items. Starbucks veered away from their focus of making coffee at the highest standards and providing this third place atmosphere for customers. During this time, Schultz walked into a Starbucks and the smell of ham wafted into his nose, rather than the smell of coffee. Can you imagine building a business off a vision of excellent coffee and not even recognizing the signature scent when visiting one of your former stores?

Schultz came back as CEO in 2008 and shut down every Starbucks for a couple of hours to retrain employees on the art of making coffee and the vision of Starbucks. When Starbucks got back to its roots and core vision, stocks and profits soared.

As a side note, and to update you on my coffee-drinking journey: It's been two years since my Dutch Bros. coffee experience, and my palate has come a long way. I'd say my number one drink is an iced white mocha from Starbucks. My wife, Kendra, is thrilled with this evolution because she basically has a Starbucks IV drip daily!

Maybe when you started reading this chapter you thought, *Oh, vision. That's like writing goals and stuff, right?* Wrong. A vision is not a goal. A VISION is not the road to success, it's the success road. A GOAL is a benchmark along the way. **When you think VISION, think, *This is where I want to see this organization go, striving toward the future.***

Here's another example in the world of sports. (I mention this lesson in my book Master Your Mindset and think it's worth revisiting.) If you've ever watched a Seattle Seahawks game, you've probably witnessed the enthusiastic demeanor of head coach, Pete Carroll. You might be surprised to learn that as a young NFL defensive backs coach for the Minnesota Vikings, Carroll's style wasn't exactly favorable. He'd often play down mistakes and tell players, "It's OK, you'll get better next time" (or something to that effect), rather than chastise them. The Vikings head coach at the time told Carroll he needed to be tough on the grown men he was coaching. This conflicted with the vision of how Carroll wanted to lead. Carroll's career continued, and when he took a head coaching job for the New York Jets, he knew how he wanted to lead—he had an idea for his vision—but he also knew it conflicted with a more hard-nosed approach the owner and general manager desired. Carroll later got fired and rehired by the New England Patriots, but the same thing happened. He got fired. He felt a lot of pressure to act and coach a certain way.

So, here's Pete Carroll in the year 2000 without a job. He started reading legendary basketball coach John Wooden's books voraciously. Carroll learned Wooden didn't win a championship at UCLA until year sixteen. SIXTEEN! By then, Wooden had created his famed "Pyramid of Success," his vision and philosophy of how he leads. Carroll started filling notebook after notebook with ideas and thoughts and summed it up with his own pyramid called "Win Forever," including his mantra of "Always Compete." He took this vision to his interview at the University of Southern California and shared it with their athletic director. Carroll was confident in his vision and approach, how he would lead and recruit. He got hired, turned the program around, won multiple national championships, and produced several Heisman Trophy winners. He never wavered in his philosophy.

His critics said he couldn't take this "Pom-Pom Pete" approach back to the NFL and be successful. But Carroll met with the Seahawks' owner, shared his vision, and got hired. He played music at practice, let players be authentically themselves, and led out of love. And you know what? It worked. It's still working. Seattle has had plenty of success under Carroll, including a Super Bowl championship. His career as a coach did not truly take off until he had his clear vision ironed out.

Now, years later, Carroll wants to spread that visionary mindset. He's teamed up with psychologist Michael Gervais to offer what they call "Compete to Create," a company created to give people and organizations the tools to be their best. They've worked with numerous elite businesses, including Microsoft. One of the foundational questions Carroll and Gervais ask is, "What is your philosophy?" Another way to say this is, what's your internal framework? If you're 100 percent sure of this, when you're hit with turbulence and walking your way through storms—or even when you're in the midst of success—you can be authentically yourself because you have no doubts about who you are and what you stand for.

MVPS

I've worked my way through Carroll and Gervais' system, and I'm a firm believer. In my personal walk with high-performance training and coaching, I've created tools to help my teams and clients create their own philosophies and unlock their vision. I call these the **MVPs: Mission, Values, Purpose, and Slogan.**

MISSION

When I started my consulting business, at the time, called Project Rise, I came up with my own MVPs. I went through this process myself so I could walk the walk as I was talking the talk. I stood at a whiteboard and started writing down all the things, beginning with my mission—or what I wanted to do right then. A mission statement briefly explains what you do and who you serve. It's often confused with a vision statement, which is more aspirational or descriptive of the future-state of your group.

When I consult with small businesses and big businesses alike, one of the first questions I ask is, "What's your mission statement?" I can't tell you how many employees have no clue. I'm shocked when leaders have to pull up their company website to read it. A mission statement is foundational and should be a hallmark of your group. Every person should know it by heart and off the top of his or her head. More importantly, if companies have a mission statement and core values, shouldn't we, as individuals, have personal mission statements . . . or at least do the work to understand what drives us and how we should show up each day?

Here's how my personal MVPs looked when I finished (we will talk more about each of these things in a bit):

MISSION: To empower the world to go for it
VALUES: Gratitude, Giving, and Growing
PURPOSE: Through my descent and my rise, give people tools to be the best version of themselves
SLOGAN: Become the best version of you #BVOY

Over the years, I've taken the MVPs a step further, and I like to ask people, "What are your three truths?" **If all of your personal content was erased, and you had to summarize your work and what you believe, what three things would you say?** Think about it for a bit. This is tough, huh? Don't overthink it, though. It doesn't have to be long.

My three truths are: To be AUTHENTIC, to be PRESENT, and to have COURAGE.

These three words serve as a guidepost for me when I get nervous if I'm about to give a presentation, or when I'm meeting someone, or when

I'm in a new environment. My only litmus test is this: Was I authentic in that moment? Was I really present and enjoying the moment, or was I worrying about past mistakes or bad things that could happen? Did I allow myself to be comfortable being uncomfortable?

Having courage is about stretching your comfort zone and facing fear. Writing a blog post, starting a podcast, speaking to groups, creating a series of videos to help people. These are things that take courage. Figuring out the three truths of your organization can help guide the creation of your MVPs, also.

VALUES

When I think of values, immediately I'm taken back to my childhood. When I was in eighth grade, I was at a high school basketball game with a bunch of my friends. I had a buddy who was a year older and had his license. He had a group of friends with a genius idea of bashing mailboxes. I knew this was so wrong, and I didn't feel comfortable. But at this age, I didn't have any sort of value system organized or a clear vision of how I wanted to conduct myself. So I went with that group of kids, and we bashed mailboxes. And you know what? I was a baseball player, so I was hitting bombs! I was the best at mailbox bashing. But we were so stupid. We were bashing mailboxes on a dead-end street. We had to drive back out of the cul-de-sac and pass the houses of the busted mailboxes. Neighbors jotted down the license plate and called the cops. A police officer happened to be on duty just three blocks away. He spotted our car and pulled us over. My heart was beating out of my chest. We tried to hide the bat under the passenger seat, and of course the police found it. They drove us down to the police station, took mugshots, fingerprinted us, and threw us in a jail cell. We had to call our parents to pick us up, and we were sentenced to several months of community service. We went to every single house and apologized. I was such a coward. I stood in the back with my head down. I had no conviction, no values, no vision.

Does this story make you think of a similar experience in your youth—hopefully not bashing mailboxes, but perhaps a time when you did something you were uncomfortable doing? You probably had a set of values you just hadn't ironed out because of your youth. As you read this, I'm sure you can rattle off some of your values now. Maybe honesty or integrity are on the list. If top companies have a mission and set values, you should, too. Confidently knowing your values makes it easier to lead your group through the process of uncovering its values, too.

If you stand for nothing, you'll fall for anything, as Alexander Hamilton so eloquently said. With clear values decisions are easy. **So what is your organization going to stand for? What are your values?** Take the time to brainstorm some specific values that will guide your behavior.

PURPOSE + SLOGAN

Here's an example of vision in action, which also couples PURPOSE with a SLOGAN, or mantra. Last winter, I got a call from Marc Wiese, the head baseball coach at Puyallup High School in Washington state (my alma mater). Wiese asked me to work with his team on mindset training and also help him, as a leader and coach, cast a vision for his program that would stand the test of time.

For starters, I developed a slideshow filled with different examples of the power of vision. I showed a video of Western Michigan University's then-head football coach, PJ Fleck, discussing his vision, which includes the mantra: "Row the Boat." You may be reading this and feel confused. What does rowing have to do with football? Well, when you're in a rowboat, you can't see where you're going because your back is facing the front of the boat. All you see is what's behind you. But rowing with teammates creates energy you build together. The boat is what Fleck calls **F.A.M.I.L.Y.**, which stands for: **F**orget **A**bout **M**e, **I** **L**ove **Y**ou.

This mantra came from Fleck's personal life, after his infant son died. He said he became determined to triumph over his tragedy by simply "rowing his boat" every day. He carried the mantra into his coaching career his first year at WMU, when he was one of the youngest coaches in the country. Even after winning just one game his first season, Fleck continued to preach "Row the Boat." The following three seasons, the Broncos celebrated winning seasons and bowl appearances, including the Cotton Bowl. Quickly they garnered top recruits and were ranked in the top twenty. After four seasons, Fleck took his mantra to the University of Minnesota, which became bowl-eligible in his second year. Fleck's vision very clearly combines his purpose of ensuring his program is a family, along with his mantra of "Row the Boat." If you haven't seen this guy in action, you should look up Fleck on YouTube and watch this video about his vision.

To keep the wheels turning regarding his team's purpose and potential slogan, I also showed Coach Wiese and his team a clip of *Hacksaw Ridge*, a movie about a real-life WWII soldier who wouldn't carry a gun based on his religious and personal beliefs. Desmond Doss had a vision of serving others through the war effort, though, and he believed he would make a difference. During a gruesome battle on a ridge (hence the name of the film), he crawled to find wounded soldiers, tied a rope around their bodies, and lowered them off the cliff to medics waiting to aid. His prayer was, "Lord, please help me get one more." He single-handedly help save seventy-five wounded soldiers with this approach. If that's not the power of vision in action, then I don't know what is.

After this clip, I broke Coach Wiese' team into groups of five. I had them write down words and phrases that they wanted other people to visualize when they think of Puyallup High School Baseball. I also asked them which brands they liked that symbolize excellence, giving examples of Amazon, Starbucks, Nike, etc. Finally, I asked them to create a slogan that embodied the program using this exercise as guidance.

As a side note: I'm guessing you've probably heard the slogan "Just Do It." Am I right? Well, in 1988, Nike was worth $900 million. They created this tagline to embody what they stood for as a company, their mission, values, and purpose—all in one—and also evoke a call to action. Nike's profits skyrocketed to $9 BILLION in a few years.

Now back to the Puyallup baseball team. We wrote all of the slogans on a whiteboard and voted on a collective favorite. The slogan they came up with was, "Just Row It." It's a combo of Just Do It and Row the Boat, as well as a nod to their mascot, the Vikings. For these guys, "Just Row It" invokes a message of "don't think, don't worry, don't stress . . . just go for it!" They made a huge banner in the outfield with that message, "JUST ROW IT," and every post on social media followed with a hashtag, #JUSTROWIT. And guess what? They won the state championship that year.

Now, I'm not going to say this vision workshop is the sole reason these guys won state, but they banded together and had a battlecry after creating their "Just Row It" slogan. And now Coach Wiese can definitively say he has a clear vision for his team.

To recap, a vision is not a goal. A vision is a future state, whereas a goal is checkpoint along the way. Developing your MVPs will help you nail down your vision in detail. Your mission is intent—what are you trying to do? Values summarize your core beliefs and what's going to guide your behavior. Purpose is your meaning or why, as we discussed in the previous chapter. What's the purpose behind your mission? And your slogan is a punchy way to tie these things together and express what you're all about. A slogan is something that people within and outside of your organization should know—your teammates, opposition, fans. Everyone should know what you stand for.

So what are your MVPs?! Clarity is power. It's amazing what happens when you have your MVPs in place. Remember: The best focus on LESS not MORE. This system simplifies your approach to creating a meaningful and succinct vision, which is the second key to creating positive culture within your group. A lot of people—a lot of teams and groups—don't sit down and put in the time to do this work.

Start by thinking about the people who inspire you. **What traits do they possess? How do you want to impact and affect others?** Write this stuff down. It's all a part of the process. Create a vision, and have an endless pursuit to be the best version of yourself . . . of your organization. It simply can't happen without a clear vision.

CULTURE CASE STUDY

///////////////////////////////////

WHO: Roger Archer

WHAT: Motion Church

WHERE: Puyallup, Washington

WHY & HOW: Roger Archer might know a thing or two about building culture. He's the senior pastor of Motion Church, which started more than twenty years ago out of his home and has grown to include three campuses and thousands of members. He's mentored and developed pastors who have gone on to plant recognizable churches across the country and has changed countless lives, including mine. His personal and church mission is to love God and love people, and he encourages others to "identify the gold you see in others that they don't see in themselves." Spend five or ten minutes with Archer, and he'll fill your head with one-liners like this, as well as scripture passages that roll of his tongue in a way you know he was made to do what he does. He's about innovation, fun, and rest, and he infuses who he is into what he does, living the Motion Church values daily. "Our values perpetually have to be an overflow of who we are. They must be who we are, not what we do because if they're not what we do, then we can't sustain them," he said. Archer has his own keys for creating winning culture, which can be condensed to three words: Love, give, forgive.

Check out Archer's explanations for each below.

1. LOVE: "The most genuine, authentic catalyst in the universe is love. Love that is selfless and promosted others will be magnetic and fragrant."
2. GIVE: "Generosity is a perpetual trampoline with infinite energy."
3. FORGIVE: "I'm going to forgive people for how they wound or hurt me."

As a leader, do you know your values? Are you living your values? Do your personal values align with the values you want your organization to stand for?

LEARN MORE ABOUT ROGER ARCHER: motionchrch.com

CHAPTER FOUR
STANDARDS

"Keep your heels, head, and standards high." —*Coco Chanel*

In 2018, I had the pleasure of conducting multiple mental conditioning sessions with the Tulane University baseball team, alongside one of my favorite humans, head coach Travis Jewett. During my time on the campus of the Green Wave, I developed a close relationship with baseball recruiting coordinator and assistant coach, Eddie Smith. We hit it off right away as we both grew up in the Pacific Northwest and share a love of leadership, personal development, and writing. Smith has since left the staff at Tulane and, at the time of publishing, coaches at Louisiana State University.

Prior to his time at Tulane, Smith was the head baseball coach at Lower Columbia College in Washington state and achieved a level of success that earned him the national coach of the year in 2015. LCC competes in the NWAC conference, which includes all of the community colleges in Washington, Oregon, Idaho, and British Columbia. The Red Devils were ranked in the top ten teams in the country for three out of the four years Coach Smith was at the helm, and they won the conference championship three of those years.

So why am I telling you about Eddie Smith? Because when asked about his success at LCC, Smith doesn't even contemplate the question. He attributed the **standards** and **expectations** of his teams that were addressed long before the first pitch of the season.

EXPECTATIONS

"I always looked at our first team meeting as one of the most important times of the year for our team—a time when general expectations of how things were run . . . to set that foundation," Smith said. "There was clarity in what we were doing. There was an understanding of what was expected out of them."

After that first meeting, Smith spent the next two to three weeks leading twenty- to thirty-minute morning meetings called "Baseball 101s," which covered specific topics that would prepare his players for situations on and off the field.

"We wanted our players to be aware of the situations and understand and have strategies to go about navigating these situations before they'd even be in them."

From small things like being on time and where to sit in class to how to handle oneself in social situations, Smith believed in developing his players into four pillars: athletics, academics, leadership, and community. And he believed a lot in accountability—out of his players, yes, but also out of himself.

"As a coach, I always felt like if I hadn't addressed it beforehand, and it happens, and I don't like it, it's my fault, it's not the players' fault." (In other words, you're either coaching the behavior or allowing it to happen.)

Smith's LCC teams met a lot, but they met with purpose, also. He kept his meetings short and succinct with the goal of having players walk away being able to "regurgitate" (as Smith said) the information in some sort of way. And with each expectation explained (what Smith hoped for his team), eventual standards were set in place—that is to say, a high caliber of performance, accountability, and pride, that translated to a winning reputation and tradition. It's also important to note that Smith's expectations came with strings attached.

"If you didn't show up on time, you'd do extra conditioning or have something taken away or would be sent home," Smith said. "You might have baseball taken away. That taught the behavior. There are serious consequences. They're in place so that we can go reach our dreams. The veterans understood and brought the rookies on along toward these expectations."

One of Smith's players somewhat jokingly called Smith's expectations and pillars the "Yellow Brick Road."

"As a coach, that was a big goal of mine—to lay down a Yellow Brick Road that if the players could just follow that, that they could be successful. Even the people who might be the most challenging in the team setting, they still want expectations at the end of the day. For any team to be successful, there's got to be clear expectations. When there's a clear expectation, that's what's going to create unity for that team."

Reader, don't you want to shout "PREACH!" after reading about Coach

Eddie Smith and his great expectations? I wanted to start off this chapter about standards with Smith's explanation of expectations because I truly don't think you can have high standards for your organization if you don't build a foundation of CLEAR expectations, which turn into standards. You want your team to have a standard of timeliness? Well, as Smith instilled, make "being on time" an expectation and establish a consequence for tardiness. Over time, the expectation will become a standard. Side note: I partnered with Coach Smith to co-author a book to help with creating a high performing team, called *Culture Toolbox for Coaches and Leaders*. This book provides 40 activities and lessons to help your team connect, establish trust, and create clear standards (available on Amazon.com).

The standards for your specific group might look different than anybody else's, but through my experience as an athlete, working professional, and coach, there are standards I believe to be essential ingredients for a winning culture: **Optimism and gratitude** (together), **service**, and **innovation**. I couple gratitude and optimism because, in my opinion, you can't have one without the other.

OPTIMISM AND GRATITUDE

In his book *The Happiness Advantage* happiness researcher Shawn Achor explains how many people think they need success first in order to be happy. *If I get that car . . . If I get the promotion . . . If I date so-and-so . . . If I earn a six-figure salary . . .* whatever it might be, *THEN I'll be happy.* Achor's years of research found that it's actually the opposite. The people who are truly happy are those who live with a spirit of optimism and gratitude. Research shows individuals with these traits are able to achieve success faster and sustain it longer. **How are you looking at the glass each day? Half-full or half-empty?**

Need more proof of the power? Check this out. The 2018 Sports Illustrated Sportsperson of the Year was the Golden State Warriors. Head Coach Steve Kerr and team won the NBA championship for three of the previous four years. And if you take a look at Kerr's four values for his team, you'll see they don't include "winning." Kerr's values are: **joy, mindfulness, compassion,** and **competition**. First of all, take note that this team actually has clear values written down. Secondly, JOY is the number one value. In my research and experience with countless teams, and of course in my own experience as an athlete, let me tell you—pessimism and any form of negativity just does not work. Optimism and gratitude lead to a joyful spirit that can accomplish great things. Things like winning championships. **How might that translate to your organization? What are your big aspirations?**

In the 1980s, MetLife (the life insurance company) expanded its salesforce. During the hiring process for new sales reps, the company separated candidates into two groups: optimists and pessimists (I know you probably have questions as to how and why they did this, but for the sake of this point, I'm going to gloss over the complexities and rationale). Interestingly, they found the pessimistic group tended to have better experience, whether that be better jobs or more education. On the other hand, the optimistic group generally lacked experience. MetLife tracked the new hires, and in their first year, optimists outsold the pessimists by 21 percent. The second year, they outsold the pessimists again, but this time by 57 percent. This radically changed how MetLife interviewed and how they hired.

The story of MetLife and the success of optimistic sales reps just hammers home the point that attitude is everything. If you fail or have setbacks or hardships—and you will because this is life, right?—but if you look at those situations through the lens of an optimist, you wouldn't cast blame, make excuses, or wonder *Why me?*. You'd ask, "How can I learn from this?" Optimists say, "Oh that happened for a reason," or "I can do it better next time." Michael Jordan was surely an optimist, as one of his most famous quotes details all the ways he's failed and concludes with "I've failed over and over and over again in my life. And that is why I succeed."

Are you an optimist by nature? If you like the idea of optimism . . . of positivity and joy, hopefulness and faith in great things . . . then it will be easy for you to translate this as a standard for your organization. If you tend to view things more pessimistically, then I encourage you to look to your most optimistic friends, colleagues, mentors, or even acquaintances and dig into how they're able to live with the glass half-full. You can't talk the talk if you're not walking the walk.

I feel like I can talk about optimism and gratitude a lot because they are so vital, and I think their benefits are often overlooked. Here's another example of their power. I mentioned author Shawn Achor and *The Happiness Advantage* earlier. In this book, Achor talks about the Nun Study (you can Google this, it's a real thing!), which followed Catholic nuns from their early twenties to their death, analyzing journal entries. Scientists were able to separate the entries from the nuns as either negative or positive. The positive nuns outlived the pessimistic nuns by almost ten years! Can you believe this?!

There's performance evidence, health benefits, and plenty more research surrounding optimism. It's not only contagious, it is scientifically proven to be beneficial. I couple optimism with gratitude because I believe the two go hand in hand. Optimism is the philosophy and perspective of expecting something good to come or something positive to come out of a situation. It's a belief and a hope. Gratitude is the act of being thankful. Being grateful is often a first step to being more confident and hopeful.

In a previous chapter, we talked a bit about my personal work success. In 2017, I was the number one sales rep in the nation for my team when I simultaneously started speaking, consulting, writing books, and working with teams and businesses on high performance training. People often asked me how I was number one, and I'd tell them my top business strategy when meeting with customers. It was these two words: **thank you.** I simply let my customers know how grateful I was for working with them and how thankful I was for what they were doing for patients. I said thank you and emphasized genuine gratitude on every single sales call. The crazy thing was that most of the people I worked with did not receive this type of thanks. As it turns out, people just don't go out of their way to say thank you. I'm someone who starts my day writing down three things I'm grateful for and thanking God for my blessings, so this was hard for me to believe. But how about you? **Are you using gratitude as a strategy to build a positive culture in your organization?**

SERVICE

Let's talk a bit about marriages or partnerships that don't last. You might not think of such relationships as culture environments, but that's exactly what they are. It really only takes two people to establish an organization or culture, right? So if you're wondering why some partnerships fail, it's not because of a lack of sex or money or whatever you might think it is. It's because expectations weren't met. If expectations aren't laid out upfront, then it creates a chain reaction that can lead to loss. If one or both of you didn't share your expectations or articulate them clearly and someone's needs aren't met, then resentment can start to creep in. Perhaps one of you thought you'd talk about your feelings but never said it aloud, and then you became disappointed. It's a chain. Expectations are kind of like rules. If no one knows the rules, then how can anyone play fair? And the same can apply to business partnerships (minus the sex aspect).

Without going down a rabbit hole of relationship expectations, I want to use this example as a way to share how important service is. Before she was my bride, my wife, Kendra, dumped me. She did. We broke up for several months. While on that break (and I knew it was a "break" because I was determined to marry her), I wrote the blueprint for our relationship. And it was all about service. If you and your partner establish the standard of service, then both of you win. If your main goal is to serve your partner, and your partner's is to serve you, then your needs will be met. It's about being selfless.

So how does this translate to the culture within your organization? Well, it's important to establish **servant leadership**. (If you're unfamiliar with the concept of "servant leadership," I encourage you to spend a bit of time researching, and you will be amazed and enlightened. It's as simple as putting others first. Also check out the Culture Case Study about John Norlin at the end of this chapter.)

I preach the **THREE Ls of SERVANT LEADERSHIP:**
1. **Love** your people (no explanation needed—all you need is love, right?),
2. **Learn** about them (know your people! That is to say, be curious so if someone is struggling or not hitting the mark you can show empathy and understanding or perhaps even insight into why they might be), and
3. **Live** in those values (don't do things out of tough love, but rather, you should "love tough" and love first. The "toughness" is loving and serving).

Think about your own relationships. **What are your habits? How are you serving?** This is a good first step into establishing expectations and then a standard of service. And if you need a visual for servant leadership, take a look at a picture of wolves traveling in a pack. One might think the wolf leading the pack is the alpha wolf. They don't say "the leader of the pack" for nothing, right? But on the contrary, the alpha wolf is in the very back. It sacrifices itself making sure every other wolf in front is safe and protected.

When I think of servant leadership, besides the wolf pack example, I think of the only time I fumbled the football during my college career. I was returning a punt against the University of Idaho, and I just dropped the ball. I ran over to the sideline, embarrassed and frustrated with my head down, and the first person to greet me on the sideline was our head coach, Mike Price. He gave me a big hug and said, "Collin, I love you, and I've got your back. You're our guy back there." Though many coaches lead out of fear, this coach just showed me empathy. It's a memory so clearly etched in my mind as the epitome of servant leadership.

If you want to look at business, how about one of my favorite examples, Amazon. I reference it a lot because Amazon focuses on so many of the right things. Its top business principle is to be obsessed with the customer. That comes down to the act of SERVICE. Amazon cares more about putting the customer first than growing market share. You can disagree with me, but have you ever had a negative experience customer service-wise with Amazon? I'd like to hear about it, if you have. Maybe you didn't like a product, but that's nothing to do with the service you received.

Service, serving, and servant leadership are about "we" and not "me." Have you ever heard a coach say, "We play for the name on the front of our jerseys and not the back?" Some teams, like Notre Dame, military academies, and even some pro teams don't put player names on their jerseys as a way of emphasizing the team over the individual. It boils down to the fact that selfishness divides, and I just have not seen a selfish team do well. Plain and simple. I encourage you to think about how you can promote service as a standard.

INNOVATION

The final standard I deem a pillar for winning cultures is innovation. Maybe that spurs images of technology or flying cars, but stick with me. I'm talking about positive changes not grand upheavals because in work, sports, and life in general, you're either growing . . . or you're dying.

The worst thing you can say as the leader of an organization is, "This is how we've always done it." Do you want some proof? Do you know that Blockbuster had the opportunity to buy Netflix years ago and passed? Blockbuster was happy with its video store model, not anticipating the way in which people watched movies would change. Now Netflix is worth billions of dollars, and Blockbuster has just one remaining store in the US, in Bend, Oregon. Similarly, MySpace had the chance to buy Facebook when it was in its infancy and didn't. Some people have never even heard of MySpace, whereas Facebook has more than 2 billion active users worldwide. And have you ever heard of Excite? Well, in the late 1990s, this search engine company could have purchased Google (yes, GOOGLE!) for $750,000, but as the story goes, the CEO didn't want to replace some of its technology with the Google search engine. Obviously each of these examples is more complex than the sentence explanation I share, but the point is, if you aren't willing to grow and change, you might miss out on a huge opportunity. Often that opportunity is greatness.

In the world of sports, the University of Alabama football team is pretty dominating. One might think head coach Nick Saban found a winning formula and has been riding the success tide since. Renown mental performance coach Trevor Moawad, who currently works with the Seattle Seahawks' Russell Wilson, used to be with the University of Alabama football team. Moawad said the reason Saban is so successful and exceptional at coaching is because he's always trying to innovate. From how his players eat and sleep to how they train their bodies and improve their mindset, Saban is constantly learning and willing to change and grow. Just as Ray Kroc, who transformed McDonald's into what it is today, said, "As long as you're green you're growing, and as soon as you ripen you start to rot."

Unless you're living under a rock, you've heard of Apple co-founder Steve Jobs, but did you know the Apple board of directors ousted Jobs in the mid-'80s? So he started the company, NeXt, and then became CEO of Pixar. Apple brought Jobs back on board in the late '90s. At the time, the company had many product offerings, but Jobs thought they should focus on the iMac, working to improve it—things like changing its color and shape. And then Jobs really started innovating, particularly in the music market. Jobs' vision helped create things that are just a part of our everyday lives now: iTunes, the iTunes platform, the Apple store, the iPod, then the iPhone, and the iPad . . . I mean, this list! It's incredible, isn't it? It's innovation at its finest.

Aren't these stories inspiring? The world changers surely don't say, "This is how we've always done it." They might have the same core values, of course, but they are open to change. They're OK with trying new things to get to the correct innovation in whatever they're doing, be it sports, technology, marriage, marketing, writing . . . it really doesn't matter the topic. And they're also OK with failing. I like to say that the word **FAIL** just stands for **F**irst **A**ttempt **I**n **L**earning. Without failure, there's no growth, and the same goes for innovation.

Try things. Be OK with change. Think about your organization and how you've been running your business or team. Does the start of every new year feel like Groundhog Day or are you open to new ideas and ways of doing things? Are you stuck in a rut or smooth sailing? Either way, think of ways you can mix things up. Variety is the spice of life, after all, right? Continue learning and growing. This doesn't mean you have to change your process every year—please don't do that. But the only constant in life is change, so embrace it, and use it to your advantage.

Hopefully all of these stories motivate you to work toward crystal clear standards for your organization. If you're not sure where to start, then begin with CLEAR EXPECTATIONS. Write down your non-negotiables and how you plan to introduce and also maybe enforce these. Think about baseball coach Eddie Smith and his beginning of the season team meeting. I truly believe optimism and gratitude, service, and innovation should be a part of your list of standards, but it's up to you to create your list, specific to your organization.

Now that you've read my suggested standards, which of these do you need to work on most? Are there any other high-performance standards you would add to the list? Regardless of which standards and values you choose to focus on, just remember to keep them clear, simple, and consistent. Because in the end, you never outperform your standards.

CULTURE CASE STUDY

/////////////////////////////////////

WHO: John Norlin

WHAT: CharacterStrong

WHERE: Based in Puyallup, Washington; implemented internationally

WHY & HOW: *"Be intentional about serving someone without expecting anything in return."* This quote would have never applied to the high school version of John Norlin, and he probably would have laughed knowing he would be the one to say it someday. As a teen, Norlin cared about himself, and he cared about hockey . . . period. He would classify himself as "indifferent." That is, until he went away to hockey camp one summer in Canada. On his first night away, a coach spoke to the group of teenagers, sharing how life was more than hockey. This coach told the group that who you are as a person is far more important than the scoreboard at the end of each day. This single concept introduced Norlin to "servant leadership" and the idea of keeping the question "how can I help?" top of mind every day. Norlin grew curious and immersed himself in leadership at the camp, heading back year after year. He took what he learned back to his high school and got involved in student-leadership. Norlin even stood at the door of his school for 180 days straight to greet people, an experience that changed his life. It gave him a desire to become an educator, and following college, he immediately started teaching high school student leadership. Even as a young teacher, his goal was to serve youth, to be impactful during the teen years. He did this through teaching the principles of servant leadership (based on the book *The Servant*, by James C. Hunter), which give students tools to handle adversity, establish character, manage social-emotional situations, and express gratitude, among countless other benefits.

Word spread about Norlin's work, and educators began reaching out to him for lessons. Three-hour meetings turned into training sessions, and eventually an annual conference was born. From the conference, the idea of a program, CharacterStrong, developed, which provides educators with curricula and trainings. In the words of CharacterStrong, these trainings help educators "focus on character development in order to help students cultivate social-emotional skills, their emotional intelligence, and help them develop a stronger identity and purpose in school and in the world." Countless lives have been touched by the work of Norlin and CharacterStrong. For Norlin, "the road to character is a constant battle," but it's important to stay focused on the little things you can do to make a difference, as well as understanding that the kind of difference you can make is entirely up to you. Everyone looks to someone else for help, and according to Norlin, "You may be 'the person' for someone and never know it."

What are the "little things" you do currently to help improve the lives of those you lead? How would you classify your leadership style? If you don't currently practice servant leadership, what's one small change you could make to move toward

a style that puts these principles into action?

LEARN MORE ABOUT CHARACTERSTRONG:

characterstrong.com

CHAPTER FIVE
LANGUAGE

"Words have great power. The power to help, the power to heal, and the power to hurt. Use this power carefully." —Anthony Douglas Williams

On September 15, 2017, I launched my first book, *Project Rise*. That same day, I gave the keynote speech at a middle school assembly. I thought it'd be fitting to share a story I often use when working with athletes. I detail a pre-game situation from one of my college football games . . . and not just any game, but a rivalry game against the University of Washington Huskies. I start telling these teenagers about how the UW marching band waltzed onto our field and started playing *their* fight song while we were trying to warm up. Completely offended and determined to protect our turf, some of my teammates and I decided to throw footballs at the band members to get them to quit. The story goes on, and there's definitely a lesson about eliminating distractions, but that's not the reason I'm recounting this to you. When I finished my speech, I thought to myself, I really crushed that! That is, until my host pulled me aside and said, "Collin, we have a problem. The band and the choir teachers are absolutely livid. We work so hard for equality and not promoting bullying and violence, and you just talked about throwing footballs at the band."

Can you put yourself in my shoes? Immediately, I felt this pit in my stomach realizing the words I said hurt feelings and insinuated that I condoned bullying. You see, I'm used to telling that story to athletes, not a mixed crowd. **I didn't know my audience.** I didn't preface that the story is not a jocks-versus-band thing. I mean, I am a lover of the arts, after all. I used to be in choir and did ballet. I honestly connect more to the arts than I do to jocks, but this was a metaphor for quieting the noise—for developing the tools to move beyond distractions in our lives—so the story made sense to me. I was too busy trying to prove this point that I didn't even stop and think about my audience.

I was in such a funk that whole book launch day. I beat myself up at the words I chose and how I lacked empathy and awareness. I had to rectify the situation, so I immediately apologized to the band teacher, who was pretty cool about the whole thing. The choir teacher . . . well, she was not happy. I gave two assemblies that day and certainly changed the opening for the second. I also donated back money to the band department to help smooth things over.

I learned a few valuable lessons: First, at some point in your career, you're going to offend someone. I put a giant check mark next to that one after this day. Secondly, a lot of times as leaders—whether on teams or in work—we don't put ourselves in other people's shoes when we speak. So now, every time I give a speech, I think about the audience first. **How are the words and my message impacting my audience in a positive way? I make it about them and not about me. Finally, I truly understood the power of words.** You'd think I would know this as a coach/speaker/writer, but it took an embarrassing situation like this to hammer home the point.

This chapter about language is a little different than the rest. It's about the words we say to ourselves, others, and the lasting impact they can have. You're well on your way to establishing a winning culture for your organization, but if you haven't given much thought to the words you choose—from the texts and emails you send to the agendas for meetings you lead and the one-on-one sessions you conduct with members of your team and everything in-between—then you simply can't expect to foster a thriving environment for those around you.

Language is a critical part of establishing culture because it becomes a defining characteristic of a team or organization. If you look at any tribe or really any group of people that spends a considerable amount of time together, they develop their own language and slang. A lot of this is a product of their environment. As a leader, you must put thought into the words you're choosing when you establish your mission, values, purpose, and slogan. If you look at words and thoughts, they influence feelings and emotions, which in turn influence our actions. So unless you establish a consistent language that's positive, honest, and possesses the characteristics you intend your group to embody, then you're starting with a disadvantage.

But there's a lot more to communication than simply words. In fact, according to researcher Albert Mehrabian, only 7 percent of communication is the words we say, whereas 38 percent is voice and tone, and a whopping 55 percent is body language. Simply being aware of these percentages is important too. How you carry yourself and how you say things rubs off on those around you, surely to those in your organization. Take for example your posture. A study from Harvard concluded that if you have an upright posture (chest up, head up), it reduces stress in your body, and it produces the confidence hormone of testosterone. So if you're going into a speech or a sales call or anywhere you need to address the group, try focusing on your posture. A straight spine is an open mind.

I could talk about language for a long time because I've experienced the power and effects of words throughout my life. But it wasn't until I dug into mental performance and mindset training that I truly analyzed past situations and realized the weight of words. Learning about language transformed my life. I want to share five topics in the realm of language and communication for you to consider, as well as a method for providing feedback for those you lead, in hopes that these concepts guide your language discovery.

POSITIVE INTENT

Remember how I told you about the job I didn't like? The one that caused me to be physically ill? Well, there's always a silver lining, right? My manager gave me a book called *Positive Intelligence* by Shirzad Chamine, which sits atop my list for transformative literature. This book taught me about the critics that live within our minds that are designed to sabotage us. I like to call these critics "mental minions" who judge, obstruct, and disrupt our thoughts. We also have two wolves in our brains (there's a lot going on up there, huh?), the negative/bad wolf and the positive/good wolf. The bad wolf is negativity, doubt, worry, and fear. It says things like "you're not good enough," "give up," and "quit." The good wolf is positivity, optimism, joy, belief, and grace. It says things like "you can do it," "let's go," and "compete."

So, which wolf wins?

I'm sure you've heard the phrase, "Thoughts become things." How about this? Energy flows where focus goes, and like attracts like. Conversely, what you resist persists. All of this means **the wolf that w ins is the one you feed.** Which wolf are you feeding . . . personally and for those around you? As a leader or even as a parent (which we'll dive into more in a bit), your team members or kids take the words you say and turn them into self-talk. Self-talk creates self-image. Do you see how language is a chain reaction? It's crazy when you think about it in this way.

Your brain is a magnet. What you think about, you attract, whether you know it or not. Therefore, **positive intent is everything**—assuming the communication you receive is coming from a positive place, that the person you're speaking to is intending something positive. The flip side of this assumption is serving, showing empathy, and checking in with others so that they, in turn, assume positive intent, too. For example, if a teammate is giving you feedback, you can assume positive intent—even if the feedback is harsh, you have a foundation of trust and can assume you're receiving the feedback from a place of care and concern.

Positive thoughts lead to positive actions, but what good comes from a negative mindset? For every negative comment you say to someone, you need to say five positive comments to combat the negative, according to psychologist and relationship expert John Gottman. It takes a lot of effort to overpower the weight of negativity. If you think about your time as a young employee or a player on a team, I bet the feedback that comes to mind first is something negative a boss or coach said to you. Am I right?

How are you leading? Do you practice positive intent?

MENTAL IMAGES

Did you know the brain thinks in pictures, not words. So if you attach can't or don't to something that you're avoiding, you're creating neural pathways directly to that which you don't want to happen. When you're coaching or leading, it's important to avoid telling the people you work with "don't" or "can't." Need an example? Say you're a golfer approaching the tee box, and your coach says to you, "Hey, don't slice it." What do you think you're going to picture in your mind? You're creating an image of slicing it. Think about setting up positive images rather than negative.

Two years ago, following my company's national sales meeting, I was on a plane flying back to the Pacific Northwest. A sales professional from my division sat down next to me. His body language looked defeated. He just didn't look engaged, happy, or like he had any energy. I said, "What's up, man, you seem kind of down." He said, "I just didn't have a great year this year, you know? All these people got accolades up on stage and earned trips, and I . . . I just didn't perform. It was stressful." In that moment, I felt like we were meant to be seatmates.

I said, "OK. I hear you. I know it's stressful. I'm curious about mindset training, and I'm a sales trainer, so tell me, what are you thinking to yourself prior to going into a sales call with a customer?" He said, *"I walk through the things I don't want to do . . . like, don't mess this part up or don't say that."* So I said, "Well, I think that's your problem. The brain thinks in pictures not words, so you're creating mental images of what you don't want to happen. The brain doesn't recognize *don't* or *can't*, so you're going into the calls and you're not as successful as you'd like because you're not creating the image or structure that you WANT to execute." He was super thankful for our little chat. I followed up about six months later, and he said he was doing so much better in his role.

Can you think of ways to help eliminate can't and don't within your organization?

CONFIDENCE

Words can create confidence, and they can also impart doubt and fear. To address this point, let's talk about the topic of parenting. What you say and how you speak to your children affects their self-talk. (If you're not a parent, simply think of the people you lead, and the same message applies.) Your intention might be one thing, but they hear something totally different. It's like a telephone game: What you say comes out your mouth and into their ears differently.

My dad is an amazing father, an incredible coach. Let me preface this story by saying my father and I have a wonderful relationship, and I wouldn't be who I am without his support and drive to help me be the best I could be. My dad played football at Washington State University and was the all-time passing leader for a time. He played professional racquetball in the '70s and '80s and endorsed racquets. He even had an advertisement in Newsweek holding one of those racquets. He was legit! My dad also was and is one of the most competitive men in the whole world. He's intense and loves to win.

This competitive nature did not impact me until I got to be about eleven or twelve. He coached me in football and basketball and a little bit of baseball. When he wasn't coaching me, I would always hear his voice from the stands. If I didn't play well or we lost, the drives home were rough. As I got older, it got worse. I felt the heaviest weight of judgment from my dad heading into my senior year of college baseball, after a not-so-great junior season.

That summer, I played in a wood bat league in the midwest. I stayed with a host family, and after a month of games, my dad flew out to watch. At this point, I was one of the top hitters in the league, batting over .300. Before my dad arrived, I went 3-4 then 4-4. I was really feeling it. Then, it all fell apart. The first game my dad watched, I went 0-4. In the next game, I went another 0-4. After my back to back games going hitless, my dad said, "I flew this far to see you get no hits? This whole year, I can count on one hand how many hits I've seen you have."

That made my heart sink. I had so much anxiety feeling the need to perform for my dad. I wanted to feel loved and validated. The stress became too much for me, so I decided to write him a letter.

Dear Dad,

I can't have you come to my games anymore.

Collin

My senior season would be the last chance I had to play games and be a part of a team and to do something for myself. I didn't want to live in fear of failure, and I just needed the weight of these expectations gone. After writing that letter, I drove to the field where we played our games, sat in the dugout, and cried for an hour at 11 o'clock at night. I just bawled my eyes out. The words my dad said cut me so hard. And you know what? He had no idea what he said had such an impact on me. He listened to my plea and with the utmost respect, didn't come to any of my games that year.

The words you say are so impactful. They drive, support, and motivate others. But if you're not careful, they can invoke fear, stress, and doubt, among other negative emotions.

The irony of this situation became apparent when I spoke at a school last fall. One of the teachers was my teammate growing up, and he told me my dad changed his life. His parents didn't have a lot of money, so my dad would pick him up and drive him to practice. My dad also gave

him a job at his health club to earn some money. This teacher's experience of my dad as a coach was totally different. Sometimes, it's just the
intensity of living up to a parent's expectations as a son or daughter. As a
parent and leader, we must remind ourselves: Is it their goal, or is it your
goal? My dad is an exceptional man. I love him very much and I know
he loves me unconditionally. That experience certainly taught both of
us valuable lessons. That's an understatement. It became a stone in the
foundation of how I lead as a parent, teacher, and coach.

As a researcher of positive psychology, I learn a lot from experts. Social
scientist and psychologist Albert Bandura has been contributing to the
field for decades, and one of his legacy concepts is that of self-efficacy,
which is another word for confidence. Bandura says there are four ways
to create confidence: 1) physically performing the action or task at hand,
2) watching someone else do it, 3) receiving positive praise from a peer
or somebody else, and 4) understanding your psychological and/or emotional state (meaning how you respond to feelings such as stress or anxiety—as opportunities or threats). Another psychologist by the name of
James Maddux also suggests a fifth way, and that's by visualizing yourself
being successful in the action or task.

I mention Bandura because his research on self-efficacy is something
I've witnessed as a peak performance coach and especially as a parent.
It really goes hand in hand with the power of words. Whether speaking
prophetically over your children with words like, "you're amazing" or
"you're kind" or "you can do hard things," or just making sure to say "I
love you so much" often, your kids will remember these things. These
words will translate to confidence and capability.

Our oldest daughter, Bellamy, started ballet last year, but she didn't want
to keep going because she was nervous. To calm her fears, my wife told
her to chew gum and focus on the act of chewing the gum rather than

worrying, but that plan didn't work as gum chewing wasn't allowed. The nerves were too much, and Bellamy just didn't want to go back. Well, it's now one year later, and she just had her first ballet class. The weekend before, I kept telling her, "You were born for ballet! Look at you: You are built like a ballerina, you can dance like one, you have a bow in your hair like a ballerina." And we went to a youth production of the Nutcracker ballet. So, like Bandura suggests, Bellamy got to see other girls her age dance like she wanted to be dancing, which gave her confidence. I got a text from my wife during Bellamy's first lesson, and she said, "You're not going to believe what Bellamy just told me as she was walking onto the floor for her first class . . . she said, 'Mom, I was born for ballet!'"

Words matter. Speak what you seek, and then see what you said. Speak it into existence. What you say to yourself and to others has power, and what you say **out loud** has ten times more power than that. Try this: Take one day and truly think about how you address those in your organization . . . or how you write your emails to your coworkers . . . or maybe even how you speak to your customers or your friends. Be mindful of your language. **Are your words positive? Do they inspire or deflate others?**

WORDS AS ANCHORS

After working with a team, I send them printable posters that say key words and statements for their lockers, dugouts, or anywhere they will see them regularly. These are simple, influencing words like "breathe," "let's go," "be authentic," "I'm born for this," or even "BEAST!" I call these "anchor words." Think about riding in a boat during a storm. If you don't have an anchor, your ship is going to get washed away. Similarly, these anchor words and statements stay anchored to who they are and their self-image.

Clemson University football coach Dabo Swinney understands anchor words. When he took over as coach, he brought two signs into his first meeting with his team. One said "BELIEVE" and the other said, "I can't," with the T crossed out. These anchor words set the stage for his expectations and also his faith in the power of words. Every season, Dabo has a word of the year. After Clemson won the national championship in 2016 in a come-from-behind win, Dabo tearfully said in an interview that he told his players they would win the game because of "love," which was his word for the season. In 2018, the team won again, and Dabo credited their word for the season, "joy." To Dabo, JOY means: Jesus, Others, Yourself, in that order. Joy! "And don't let anyone steal it," Dabo said. Do you have anchor words or statements that help drive action? Revisit your core values from Chapter 3.

RESET BUTTON

What about those times you're stuck, and no matter how hard you try with your words or actions you just don't seem to be able to get through to your organization? Or maybe you're dealing with adversity. Whatever the setback, I think it's vital to have a plan in place and learn how to press the reset button. Time is valuable, and you're not going to want to waste the time you have to impact your team. It's important to have direction and intent in your dialogue with your team.

I teach what I call the RESET, REFOCUS, RISE system with bracelets when I do workshops with schools, corporations, and teams. You know those little rubber bracelets that people wear for different causes? Well, mine has a triangle logo on it with the mantra "RESET-REFO-CUS-RISE." When faced with adversity, here's how to use this system: First, you take a breath and say a reset word or mantra that creates action and gives you power and confidence (something like "strength" or "I can"). Then, the next step is to get your thoughts back on track, to shift your focus back to the function or task and not respond with aggression, fear, or anger. The final step is to rise. Adversity and hardship are invitations to rise, to get better, and to grow. Think about your team or organization and how you can initiate a simple system like this. Come up with some sample situations or examples of adversity and role play how you'll reset, refocus, and rise.

I taught a class last winter to a group of athletes. Weeks later, I got an email from a parent, which was actually forwarded from a teacher describing a situation involving the parent's daughter, Mary. One day at school, Mary's classmate started giving a speech but almost immediately stopped as she got so anxious and nervous. This classmate got stuck on her words and in a moment of panic, ran out of the classroom. Feeling for her classmate, Mary raised her hand and told her teacher she just sat through a training about resetting and how to deal with failure and stress and wanted to go talk to the classmate. Finding her classmate in the girls' bathroom, Mary took off her RESET-REFOCUS-RISE bracelet and handed it to her. She said, "You're being so hard on yourself. I know you're thinking worst-case scenarios and that everyone is judging you, but just press the reset button. Just take a deep breath, and say some nice things to yourself like, 'Everyone makes mistakes. I'm getting better,' and refocus your thoughts on these words." Mary then told her classmate she believed in her and went back into the classroom. A short time later, her classmate returned and finished the speech. Mary's teacher said in her twenty-five years of teaching she had never seen a student help a fellow student come back and finish something like that after being embarrassed and down on herself.

As leaders and team members, we need to coach people up, just like this. We need to step in and encourage them instead of allowing things to snowball and get worse. The top performers are able to bounce back and recover from failure and setbacks. Setbacks are not roadblocks, they are building blocks to learn and grow. Social psychologist Heidi Grant calls this type of preparedness an "if-then" plan. For example, "If I get anxiety, then I'm going to reset, refocus, and rise to the occasion." Grant says this type of thinking improves goal attainment by 300 percent. It's having a plan with your language and your actions. Thoughts become things, after all.

THE CHEESEBURGER METHOD

There's a final strategy I want to share with you, as a tool for those inevitable times you need to provide feedback. You know how we talked about energy vampires and energy zombies? What can we do regarding language? How can we be energy heroes in this regard? When you need to engage others, or if someone on your team is underperforming, and you need to provide some feedback, I believe taking a layered approach is the most effective way. I call this the Cheeseburger Method.

Side note: In the heat of the moment, there is not time for a layered approach. I get that. Sometimes you have to give instant feedback. This method, however, is for times when consistent performance reviews are required or if someone is sucking the energy out of the team and their behavior needs to be addressed for the sake of the group.

First, **open with something positive** (if you start by saying, "You're not doing a great job," you've already put your audience on the defensive). This is the first bun. Examples: "Your most recent report was so well-written." "You're doing a fantastic job enrolling new members." "I can tell you've been practicing your pull-up jumper—it looks incredible."

Next, think about the feedback you want to give. *Remember: Never say "but" as you transition to the critical feedback as it immediately negates the positive you just shared.* Let's say you need to tell someone their sales numbers aren't hitting the mark. You can get vulnerable and **share how you've had to deal with something similar**, or you can **tell a story of someone else and what happened to them**. These stories are the toppings on the cheeseburger. "When I was a rep like you, my first quarter wasn't where I'd hoped, either. I learned a ton, though, and made several key corrections like routing and use of better questioning."

The meat of the conversation (pun intended!) is the **actual feedback**. Think about using "I feel" statements instead of "you," as no one can argue with your feelings, and this approach is not accusatory. If applicable, try weaving in a "next time" scenario. This gives reassurance that there will be a next time and also that the feedback is all a part of the process. "For us to have a trusting and positive environment, we need your body language and engagement to improve. I feel your focus is not with the group, and it's affecting others. Next time, please keep your phone on silent and in your backpack."

Finally, **close with something positive**. This is the bottom of the bun. It's like opening with something positive. It is the last thing whomever you're giving feedback to will hear and it's always good to end on a high note. "You're our go-to guy on defense!"

You've already read the Culture Case Study about Pastor Roger Archer's church. Archer is a wonderful mentor and friend of mine who gives feedback almost daily. He has his own formula, which is not unlike the Cheeseburger Method, and likes to close with a prompt to ensure there's no confusion about the feedback given: "Tell me what you heard me say." This is kind of like ordering the cheeseburger again so both parties know what they're getting.

If you've ever felt unsure about your approach to giving feedback, then I suggest giving the Cheeseburger Method a try. Of course, this is NOT an absolute approach to providing feedback; merely, it's a suggestion, and one way I've found to be very helpful. It's important to take each situation and person into context. How well do you know this person to whom you're about to provide feedback? The point is to take a positive approach to uplift and inspire, while also teaching.

Another side note: There are countless feedback approaches that suggest a similar manner. In his book *Culture Code*, which explores secrets to highly successful groups, author Daniel Coyle references a particular line in which to open a feedback session: *"I am giving you these comments because I have very high expectation and I know that you can reach them."* According to Coyle, this sentence gives the recipient confidence that he or she is a part of a special group with high standards that he or she is able to meet. In other words, this sentence gives the recipient faith that he or she is safe. Think about whether or not this type of approach could work the people you lead.

The Cheeseburger Method is all about language. Try role playing this with the people in your organization. It might feel silly (I mean, it's called the Cheeseburger Method, right?!), but it's a system for dealing with things, which adds a level of preparedness and confidence for facing adverse situations. I think it's worth mentioning that it's difficult to give feedback if you haven't connected and spent time with each individual on your team. In other words, because you haven't established trust or created a foundation of positive intent, you have not earned the right to give constructive feedback.

I know I shared quite a lot about language in this chapter, but it's vital information. Some people choose their course of study or career path based off encouraging words they received when young. As an athlete, student, and sales professional, I never stopped to think about my words, but I can vividly picture coaches, leaders, and managers whose words left marks on me, for better and for worse. When you decide to put emphasis and effort into the words you say to your organization (and how you say these words), you will be astounded in the outcome, and you'll likely see positive results in yourself, also.

WHO: Jen Greeny

WHAT: Washington State University Head Volleyball Coach

WHERE: Pullman, Washington

WHY & HOW: Successful athletes often become coaches when their playing days are over. Some walk into victorious programs while others must create—or in Jen Greeny's case, "re-create"—winning cultures. Greeny was a standout hitter and blocker for the Washington State University volleyball program in the '90s, and after graduation, she became an assistant for the Cougs. Greeny played and coached during some of the most prominent years for the WSU volleyball team, so to say she knew what a winning culture felt like would be an understatement. Greeny left her assistant seat for a handful of years to begin an accomplished head coaching career at the high school level and then at Lewis-Clark State College, which competes in the NAIA division. During this time, the Cougars experienced a couple of coaching changes and an inconsistent record. They needed a revival and offered Greeny a chance to lead the program.

In taking the head coaching job, Greeny's goal was to reestablish winning habits and promote a culture of passion in Pullman. Since she coached Division I and then at the high school and small college level, Greeny said she knew how to do just about everything in the way of running a program, which gave her an advantage in understanding how to lay the foundation for a winning culture. She said it started with recruiting and sharing a consistent message with every young woman interested in playing for the Cougs. Other key ingredients, in Greeny's opinion, are time (knowing the type of culture she envisioned wouldn't happen overnight), assembling the right team leaders, and the ability of her coaching staff to share constant feedback.

Greeny's program lives by five main values, which she said she "stole" from former WSU Men's Basketball coaches Dick and Tony Bennett. Tony Bennett now coaches at the University of Virginia and won the 2019 NCAA Championship with a team rooted in these principles: **passion, unity, servanthood, thankfulness, and humility.** At the beginning of every season, her team discusses these values, placing them into real life situations both on and off the court. For example, servanthood can look like stepping up to help a teammate get extra reps outside of practice, but it can also show itself as offering to take a teammate to the store who doesn't have a car. The players are a part of the process, understanding how life is much bigger than the game of volleyball. Greeny and her staff also stress "attitude and effort" in all aspects of life.

Without a second thought, Greeny said the most important value for her program is passion. "Whatever you're doing . . . it's going to be difficult for you to be successful at anything that you're doing in life and create that culture without passion. It's hard to be thankful if you don't have passion about it. It's harder to have servanthood if you're not passionate about it. But if you're passionate about your team and your culture, your job, or whatever, then those things are easy. It doesn't seem like a job."

With passion—not to mention decades of hard work and discipline—Jen Greeny's Cougars certainly returned to dominance, including NCAA Championship Tournament appearances the past three years and a trip to the Sweet Sixteen during the 2018 season.

Is there one value you hold above all others? Can you help those you lead apply this to your organization and also to the greater picture of life? How can you inspire values that translate outside of your group?

CHAPTER SIX
LEGACY

"What we do for ourselves dies with us. What we do for others and the world remains and is immortal." —*Albert Pine*

The date was June 21, 2012. It was Game 5 of the 2012 NBA Finals. My eyes were glued to the TV. If LeBron and the Miami Heat defeated the Oklahoma City Thunder, confetti would fall, and they'd be poppin' bubbly as NBA champions. I felt the excitement of this potential series-ender during the game. Imagine my shock when my wife walked in front of the screen to tell me she was in labor. I ran and grabbed the timer to check her contractions and drew her a warm bath. I laugh about my cluelessness now, but I had my head on a swivel checking the score of the game while she was in the early stages of labor. The doc said this part would take a while, right? But as soon as things progressed, we jetted to the hospital.

Kendra made it far enough along to receive an epidural, and after watching that ten-inch needle get injected, I waited for her to get some relief.

Except she didn't. You see, the doctor didn't hit the right spot. Kendra was numb from the waist up, not the waist down. Her numbers on those beeping machines were off the charts. Just think of any epic scene from Grey's Anatomy or any of those hospital dramas. We were living this. "Why is this hurting?!" she screamed. She needed oxygen. It was getting more and more dramatic. I started panicking. I didn't know what was happening.

The baby's heartbeat and blood pressure shot up and down, and we watched, not knowing what anything meant since this was our first baby. Thankfully, Kendra got to the point where she could push, and we soon heard the words, "It's a boy!" I tried holding it together a little bit, but at this point, I just lost it. I almost couldn't breathe because I cried so hard. The rush of emotion could not and cannot be explained in words. Two people entered the hospital, and now there were three of us.

Seeing my wife go through that labor, watching as our plan to get an epidural foiled, experiencing the intensity of the situation . . . well, quickly none of that mattered as the nurses hurriedly pulled our son from Kendra. He was blue and wasn't crying. I heard someone say, "Code Blue" over the loudspeaker. I saw a rush of nurses flood into the room. I watched as they put a breathing apparatus over his face and resuscitated his body. It seemed like the longest two minutes of my life. I kept saying, "Lord, please help him cry. Please cry. Please cry." I just said that over and over. Then, I begged, "Lord, if you can save our son, if you can be present in this moment, I feel a calling that my life is bigger than me. I'm going to serve. I'm going to do something great."

Then BOOM.

"Waaaaaahhhhhh."

Baylor started crying.

In that moment, I KNEW I had to leave a legacy for my wife and my child.

LEGACY MOMENT

In Jon Gordon's book *The Power of Positive Leadership*, he reports the reflections of people in their eighties and nineties. With much life behind them, Gordon wonders if they would have done anything differently. Three common themes emerged. People said they would have 1) taken more risks, 2) focused more on experiences versus material things like houses or cars, and 3) thought more about legacy—leaving something behind bigger than themselves.

I don't need to live until I'm eighty to recognize the need for legacy. Watching my newborn son suffer and come to life proved to be a pivotal moment for me. I meant what I said to God, and that experience planted the seed for what I'm doing now as a mental performance coach. I started Project Rise in 2016 to create a movement with ripple effects that will last longer than me. Legacy is about making an impact. It's about contributing to a movement, system, or anything that seems bigger than yourself.

Most likely, you've had a legacy moment, and if you haven't, you probably will. Take a second to think about your life. **Can you relate to what's mentioned in Gordon's book and what those people in their latter stages of life said about regret? Or are you working toward some type of legacy right now?** It could be a movement you're tied to or a group you're connected to—something you're dedicated to serving and also wanting to leave a positive trail behind you. **How do you impart this hope and calling on your group**

or organization? Much like everything you've already read, this key is about modeling the behavior first and sincerely living it. As writer Chuck Palahniuk said, "We all die. The goal isn't to live forever, the goal is to create something that will."

HEROES

Have you ever taken a hard hit in life? I can think of a few hits I took while playing football at WSU. One was my freshman year against the University of Oregon, on the last play of the game. I caught an out-route pass and got hit in the ribs. The ball popped out, and the Ducks caught it, returning it for a touchdown. The fans thought the game was over and rushed the field. I lost my breath for two minutes, and when I came to, I saw our head coach, our trainer, and . . . my mom?! *Mom, what are you doing on the field?*, I thought. I can imagine my teammates: *"What is this, little league? With your mom coming on the field, Collin?"*

I took another hard hit as a slot receiver in practice. During a blitz pick-up drill, I caught a slant pattern, and the weak-side linebacker, Steve Gleason—who went on to play in the NFL—hit me so hard I saw stars. You're supposed to just wrap up the offense in this non-contact drill, but the linebacker ignored that. You know that phrase, "You got your bell rung?" Well, my ear rang for literally two hours after that hit. When we watched it back on film, I saw myself horizontal in the air. But I jumped back up after the hit, and I smacked my teammate on the butt like I was tough. Yet with every step I took I thought, *That hurt so bad.* He really rocked me.

That physical hard hit and its impact was nothing compared to the news that Gleason received in 2011 when he was diagnosed with amyotrophic lateral sclerosis (ALS), or Lou Gehrig's disease. Gleason could have quit, crumbled, raised a white flag, and given up hope, making it all about himself. But his response was quite the opposite. His mantra became "No white flags," and he started an organization called Team Gleason to help raise awareness and money to serve people living with ALS. Rather than contributing to funding for the cure to ALS, Gleason wanted to help people who were actually living with the disease. It's not what happens to you in your life, it's about your response, right?

Just as Gleason received his diagnosis, he and his wife got pregnant with their first child. They decided right then and there that they would document as many moments, memories, and lessons as possible for their son since Gleason likely would lose his ability to speak before his baby's birth. His story became a movie, *Gleason*, which you can find on Amazon Prime, and I highly recommend. I actually put off watching this film for almost a year because I was scared. I didn't have the courage to watch one of my heroes go through what he did and does. When I finally watched it, I thought to myself, I am doing nothing. To see his vision, service, humility, and to see the purpose and legacy he envisioned just inspired me to the core. For his courage, as well as for the legacy he's leaving in his foundation, Gleason received the Congressional Gold Medal in December 2018. He's the first player in the NFL to win this highest honor Congress can give a civilian. He was my teammate, he is my friend, and he will forever be my inspiration.

Do you have a hero? Someone who inspires you to do something positive or make life bigger than yourself? These are the questions you can encourage your organization or team to think about. You don't have to be well-known or famous, though there are plenty of powerful people who do lots of good for the world around them. To name a few: actor Matt Damon co-founded Water.org, whose mission is to bring water and sanitation to the world. And what about Oprah? More than ten years ago, she built the Oprah Winfrey Leadership Academy to serve underprivileged girls in South Africa. This media mogul also founded the Angel Network, which partners with other organizations and has built more than fifty-five schools across the globe. And I'm sure you've heard of Tesla founder, Elon Musk. He founded SpaceX with the goal of building a self-sustaining city on planet Mars. These celebrities are leaving legacies far beyond their contributions to their respective industries.

YOU DON'T NEED A TITLE

He might be a little lesser known, but one of my favorite examples of legacy is legendary NAIA college football coach Frosty Westering. Maybe you've heard of him or maybe you haven't, but talk to any guy who played for Frosty—whether in his early days at Parsons and Lea colleges or during his long run at Pacific Lutheran University from 1972-2003, and you'll leave with a pocketful of Frosty-isms and insight into this unorthodox coach whose strategies proved not only to be successful but life-changing for his players. For Frosty, the actual game of football was less important than the people playing, and helping shape and guide his players into upstanding men was his life's calling. He infused a lot of fun, games, and memories into each practice and in games, too. With 305 career wins, I'd say he knew what he was doing, even if it looked silly sometimes.

Frosty wrote a book detailing his style called *Make the Big Time Where You Are*. He prescribed to many cliches and told anecdotes that continue to inspire leaders. To Frosty, you didn't need a title to be a leader, and he said the "big time" wasn't a destination but a place in your heart. Yes, a lot of people called him unconventional, but he knew who he was and he knew his legacy. If Frosty's message speaks to you, you can easily adapt this legacy for your organization. Simply put, it's about **person over player or professional**. If you think about the best leaders you've worked for or with, and I bet you can recall the way they made you feel and how much they cared about you versus how well you did on the job. **Did your favorite mentor teach you more about your craft or about life?** Just think about this for a bit.

I encourage you to start by asking those you are leading what they're called to be and how they're working to be the best version of themselves for that calling. The great Martin Luther King Jr. said the following: "If a man is called to be a street sweeper, he should sweep streets even as Michelangelo painted, or Beethoven composed music or Shakespeare wrote poetry. He should sweep streets so well that all the hosts of heaven and earth will pause to say, 'Here lived a great street sweeper who did his job well.'"

As part of my family legacy, I started asking my kids two simple questions to inspire the belief that we're made for more:

Me: "Who are we?"
Kids: "Hendersons!"
Me: "And what do we do?"
Kids: "Help!"

Just like Frosty said about making the big time where you are, it's all about being the best person you can be in your role. I ask my kids every night who they helped. They know they're going to get asked this, so they have their eyes open for opportunities to help throughout the day. It's always fun to hear what they have to say—it could be as simple as helping a sister or a classmate.

Even if you're leading someone who feels stuck in their current job or position (say they're on the scout team and not a starter), coaching to change perspective and motivating someone to excel in their current situation can unlock inspiration, as well as open the door for uncovering legacy. For some, legacy is an afterthought or it's something they think about leaving behind, but I challenge you to look for a legacy moment in your life. As a leader of an organization, know that you have the ability to impart all of this knowledge onto your group. Take some time and think about where you've been and where you are going. If you're tied up in yourself and unable to acknowledge a legacy moment in your own life, think about how you want those you are leading to remember the time you're spending together.

I really could have started this book with this chapter on legacy first, as focusing on this has transformed my own life. It's made me a better partner, father, friend, neighbor, co-worker, and more. But it started with a moment, and I worked on one thing at a time. Like many of the other keys to winning culture, your legacy has a chain reaction far beyond your ability to predict. All it takes is one step to head in the right direction.

Here's a simple question to ponder and help you gain clarity: **What's your legacy and the legacy of your organization or team?** Start today what you'll wish you'd started years from now.

CULTURE CASE STUDY

///

WHO: Severson Family

WHAT: Family Business, Centrex Construction

WHERE: Portland, Oregon

WHY & HOW: Even though their entrepreneurial dad created a successful construction company from scratch, brothers Jimmy and Tom Severson, along with their sister Heather, were never intentionally steered in the direction of the family business. Rather, their father went to great lengths to fostered their individual curiosities. Jimmy grew interested in aviation, so Jim Sr. took up flying lessons with his son, and the two enjoyed it so much Jim later purchased an aircraft and began constructing airplane hangars as part of his business. Heather was into horses, so her parents nurtured this love with lessons and eventually a horse of her own to train. And Tom will tell you he was into tinkering, so his dad built an elaborate workshop in their basement to serve as his playground. Aside from the fun they shared, their dad instilled the same expectations and values in his children as he did his business: grit, unmatched work ethic, and the power of earnest relationships. These foundational qualities afforded not only a winning culture in their family and business but fostered a lasting legacy of Jim's work.

After careers in home remodeling and aviation respectively, Tom and Jimmy returned home to work for their father who passed away in 2016. To this day, the brothers use their father's values as cornerstones for their business, genuinely treat their employees as family and clients as valued friends, and approach business developments as opportunities to serve and fulfill dreams. These qualities create a construction company unlike any other, which goes above and beyond for its clients to ensure each job is done with remarkable precision and care.

Like the Severson family, how can you promote individuality and foster relationships with those you lead, especially those in your family? Have you taken time to build trust and empathy by really getting to know the people in your organization? Do you know the strengths of your team members and how you can help build up these skills?

LEARN MORE ABOUT THE CENTREX STORY: centrex.cc

CLOSING

THE KEYS

If you flip back through this book, which section has the most notes, underlining, or highlighter marks? Aside from the key transformation equation (connection + trust + vulnerability = transformation), which of the five keys to creating winning culture felt the most applicable to your organization right this minute? My advice is to turn back to that chapter and start right there.

I shared these keys in a particular order, but maybe you feel your group is crushing it in the communication department but perhaps lacking energy or even fun. If you're a coach with a team of leaders, gather these folks first, and dig into the material together. Look back at the questions posed and give everyone an opportunity to answer for themselves, as well as provide feedback to you (they can practice using the Cheeseburger Method!). Create a checklist of sorts, as well as ideas and a plan for implementing some of the practices and suggestions mentioned in each chapter.

97

Let's circle back to the Culture Killers mentioned in the beginning of this book. I asked you which of the following resonated most with your organization: ego, comparison, excuses, laziness, lack of communication, or lack of trust. Or was there possibly another Culture Killer infecting (yes, like a disease!) and affecting your team? I'm sure some of these came to mind as you read through the chapters. I hope you feel like you were given tangible tools to combat these Culture Killers. Undoubtedly, it will benefit your organization if you bring attention to these Culture Killers as things that can deflate a smooth-moving tire, or in your case, a successful, functioning team.

I firmly believe bringing energy, casting a vision, creating standards, understanding the power of language, and leaving a legacy are the five keys that will reshape your organization from a group of people working together for a common goal to a thriving culture whose work will be remembered for generations to come.

There is magic in these keys, and I can't wait to hear how it changes you and those you lead!

REFERENCES & RESOURCES

This book could not have been created without outstanding and informative work from other brilliant thinkers, researchers, and practitioners in the field of high performance.

The following four books deeply influenced me and are great follow-up reads for those looking to improve culture:

1. *The Culture Code: The Secrets of Highly Successful Groups*, by Daniel Coyle
2. *Extreme Ownership: How U.S. Navy SEALs Lead and Win*, by Jocko Willink
3. *You Win in the Locker Room First: The 7 C's to Build a Winning Team in Business, Sports, and Life*, by Jon Gordon and Mike Smith
4. *Above the Line: Lessons in Leadership and Life from a Championship Program*, by Urban Meyer and Wayne Coffey

Below is a list of sources that I either cited directly, inspired my thought process, or helped me create my own philosophy and theories that I share in this book. Some of the information shared has been absorbed in conferences or through stories shared. Regardless, I've made a tremendous effort to give credit where exceptional credit is due.

Achor, Shawn. *The Happiness Advantage: How a Positive Brain Fuels Success in Work and Life*. New York: Currency, 2010.

Akhtar, Miriam. "What is Self-Efficacy? Bandura's 4 Sources of Efficacy Beliefs," Positive Psychology.org.UK. November 8, 2008. http://positivepsychology.org.uk/self-efficacy-defini tion-bandura-meaning/

Blair, Elizabeth. "The Real 'Hacksaw Ridge' Soldier Saved 75 Souls

Without Ever Carrying A Gun," NPR. November 4, 2016.
https://www.npr.org/2016/11/04/500548745/the-real-hack
saw-ridge-soldier-saved-75-souls-without-ever-carrying-a-gun

Chamine, Shirzad. *Positive Intelligence: Why Only 20% of Teams and
Individuals Achieve Their True Potential AND HOW YOU CAN
ACHIEVE YOURS*. Austin: Greenleaf Book Group Press, 2012.

Cuddy, Amy J.C., Caroline A. Wilmuth, and Dana R. Carney. "The
Benefit of Power Posing Before a High-Stakes Social
Evaluation." Harvard Business School Working Paper, No.
13-027, September 2012. http://nrs.harvard.edu/urn-3:HUL.
InstRepos:9547823

Danner, Deborah D., David A. Snowdon, and Wallace V. Friesen.
"Positive Emotions in Early Life and Longevity: Findings from
the Nun Study," American Psychological Association. https://
www.apa.org/pubs/journals/releases/psp805804.pdf

Duhigg, Charles. "What Google Learned from its Quest to
Build the Perfect Team," New York Times. February 25, 2016.
https://www.nytimes.com/2016/02/28/magazine/what-goo
gle-learned-from-its-quest-to-build-the-perfect-team.html

Frank, Robert. "Richest 1% Now Owns Half the World's Wealth,"
CNBC. November 14, 2017. https://www.cnbc.
com/2017/11/14/richest-1-percent-now-own-half-the-worlds-
wealth.html

Frankl, Viktor E. *Man's Search for Meaning*. Boston: Beacon Press, 1959.

Gallo, Carmine. "How Starbucks CEO Charles Schultz Inspired us

to Dream Bigger," Forbes. December 2, 2016. https://www.
forbes.com/sites/carminegallo/2016/12/02/how-starbucks-
ceo-howard-schultz-inspired-us-to-dream-bigger/#3571de
dae858

Gordon, Jon. *The Power of Positive Leadership: How and Why Positive Leaders Transform Teams and Organizations and Change the World.* New Jer
sey: John Wiley & Sons, Inc., 2017.

Grant, Heidi. "Get Your Team to Do What It Says It's Going to
Do," Harvard Business Review. May 2014. https://hbr.
org/2014/05/get-your-team-to-do-what-it-says-its-going-to-do

Harvard Second Generation Study, Grant and Glueck Study, http://
www.adultdevelopmentstudy.org/grantandglueckstudy

Hood, David. "Love. Legendary. Two Words that Led to a National
Championship," TigerNet. July 25, 2017. https://www.tiger
net.com/story/Love-Legendary-Two-words-that-led-to-a-Na
tional-Championship-16028

"How Corporate Culture Affects the Bottom Line," Duke University
Fuqua School of Business. November 12, 2015. https://www.
fuqua.duke.edu/duke-fuqua-insights/corporate-culture

Keenan, Jim. "The Proven Predictor of Sales Success Few are Using," Forbes. December 5, 2015. https://www.forbes.com/s
ites/jimkeenan/2015/12/05/the-proven-predictor-of-sales-
success-few-are-using/#56244bb4ede6

Mineo, Liz. "Good Genes are Nice, but Joy is Better," Harvard Ga
zette. April 11, 2017.

https://news.harvard.edu/gazette/story/2017/04/over-near ly-80-years-harvard-study-has-been-showing-how-to-live-a-healthy-and-happy-life/

Moesgaard, Simon. "4 Ways to Develop Self-Efficacy Beliefs," Reflectd co. January 20, 2014. http://reflectd. co/2014/01/20/self-efficacy-beliefs/

"NCAA Recruiting Facts," NCAA.org. March 2018. https://www. ncaa.org/sites/default/files/Recruiting%20Fact%20Sheet%20 WEB.pdf

"Optimism = Sales Success." Metropolitan Life Case Study. https:// studylib.net/doc/8273743/metropolitan-life-case-study

The Season 2019. "The Season 2019 'Miami RedHawks' - Chapter 1 New Beginnings," YouTube. October 4, 2018. https://www. youtube.com/watch?v=_tu1GDO-g5Y&t=3s

Thompson, Jeff. "Is Nonverbal Communication a Numbers Game? Is body language really over 90% of how we communicate?" Psychology Today. September 30, 2011. https://www.psychologytoday.com/us/blog/ beyond-words/201109/is-nonverbal-communication-num bers-game

Zak, Paul J. "The Neuroscience of Trust," Harvard Business Review. January-February 2017. https://hbr.org/2017/01/the-neuro science-of-trust

ABOUT THE AUTHORS

Collin Henderson is a peak performance coach in the fields of athletics, business, and academics. He is an author, speaker, sales trainer, and mental conditioning consultant for a plethora of professional and amateur athletes, as well as business professionals.

He received his undergraduate degree in sports management, with an emphasis in business, and his master's in education from Washington State University. He was a standout starter in football and baseball—in which he was a captain, Pac-12 champion, and Academic All-American.

He has spent more than a decade as an award-winning, top-ranked territory manager and sales trainer with two Fortune 500 medical sales companies.

Collin, his wife Kendra, and their five children live in the suburbs of Seattle, Washington.

Visit thecollinhenderson.com for more content, information, books, videos, and tools to improve your performance.

Instagram and Facebook: @CollinHenderson

Kate Benz Bethell is a freelance writer and editor with a background in journalism. A former collegiate athlete and coach with experience in news production, publishing, agency and corporate writing, Kate wears many professional hats. She lives in Portland, Oregon with her husband and children.

Made in the USA
Columbia, SC
11 May 2023

16445623R00064